Increase Your Score in
3 MINUTES a Day
SAT
Essay

Also in this series

Increase Your Score in 3 Minutes a Day: SAT Critical Reading,
McCutcheon and Schaffer

Increase Your Score in
3 MINUTES a Day

SAT
Essay

RANDALL MCCUTCHEON AND JAMES SCHAFFER, PH.D.

McGraw·Hill

New York   Chicago   San Francisco   Lisbon   London   Madrid   Mexico City
Milan   New Delhi   San Juan   Seoul   Singapore   Sydney   Toronto

Library of Congress Cataloging-in-Publication Data

McCutcheon, Randall, 1949–.
    Increase your score in 3 minutes a day. SAT essay / Randall McCutcheon and James
Schaeffer ; with a foreword by Arthur Golden.
        p.   cm.
    ISBN 0-07-144042-9 (alk. paper)
    1. English language—Composition and exercises—Examinations—Study guides.
    2. Scholastic Assessment Test—Study guides.

    LB1631.5 .M33   2004
    78.1'662—dc22   2004052409

9 10 11 FGR/FGR 0 9

ISBN 0-07-144042-9

Interior design by Cheryl McLean
Interior illustrations:
Page xiv by David Ernest Lyon
Page 8 © The New Yorker Collection 1987 J. B. Handelsman from cartoonbank.com. All
rights reserved.
Page 16 © 2003 ZITS Partnership. Reprinted with special permission of King Features
Syndicate.
Pages 37 and 53 © 1974. Peanuts reprinted by permission of United Feature Syndicate,
Inc.
Page 64 © 1972. Peanuts reprinted by permission of United Feature Syndicate, Inc.
Page 82 © The New Yorker Collection 2001 Danny Shanahan from cartoonbank.com. All
rights reserved.
Page 92 © Sidney Harris. Reprinted with permission.
Page 111 © 1998 ZITS Partnership. Reprinted with special permission of King Features
Syndicate.
Page 116 Calvin and Hobbes © 1993 Watterson. Reprinted with permission of Universal
Press Syndicate. All rights reserved.

McGraw-Hill books are available at special quantity discounts to use as premiums and
sales promotions, or for use in corporate training programs. For more information, please
write to the Director of Special Sales, Professional Publishing, McGraw-Hill, Two Penn
Plaza, New York, NY 10121-2298. Or contact your local bookstore.

This book is printed on acid-free paper.

....

For my grandmother
—Randall McCutcheon

....

*To Mary Lynn, for her unwavering love
and support, and to Suzanne, Sarah, and
Stephen, who make it all worthwhile.*
—James Schaffer

Contents

Foreword

Memoirs of a Grammarian

· ·

Professional writers know a secret. I'll tell it to you right now so you can skip years of ineffective writing and get directly to the effective stuff. Here goes:

Context is everything.

I know it doesn't sound like much, but you'd be surprised how few people, even very literate people, understand it. That beautiful passage you think about so often? Probably it isn't beautiful because of the writer's choice of words so much as because it draws together, and draws upon, the material that comes before it. Writing effectively isn't all that much different from telling a good joke. Rambling along during the setup only makes the punch line less punchy.

Here's another thing about context: the way you write depends on what you're writing. Advertising copy doesn't read like a novel. A novel doesn't read like a corporate report—or at least a good one doesn't.

I'm sure that right now the SAT essay makes the short list of threatening and unavoidable ordeals looming in your immediate future. Fortunately you are holding in your hand a book that, while it may not succeed in making the essay any more avoidable, can certainly make it less threatening. It is filled with reliable advice about keeping your essay on track, ensuring that things go well together, and choosing an approach suited to the task you're undertaking—in short, about being mindful of context. That, after all, is the key to effective writing.

And remember this: no matter how bleak things look, you'll still have it better than I did. I needed nine years and two discarded 750-page drafts to write *Memoirs of a Geisha*. Your struggle, on the other hand, will draw to a close no more than a few hours after it begins. Sigh.

Anyway, it's a good thing you have this wise and useful book to help you with it. So what are you waiting for? You've got some reading to do.

—Arthur Golden, author of
Memoirs of a Geisha

Acknowledgments

Ｔhe authors would like to thank the following people:
Jane Durso, Peter Durso, Elizabeth Durso, Nick Durso, Matthew Barrett, Amaris Singer, Ladan Jafari, Molly Dunn, Yasmin Mashhoon, Reah Johnson, Austan Goolsbee, Jeremy Mallory, Christopher Brown, Mary Schafer, Thomas Schaffer, Devin Bethune, Cynthia Brazda, Ashley Buck, Melissa Casper, Valerie Cobb, Gordon Coffin, Brandon Fisher, Bobbi Kracl, Dustin Lottman, Melissa McCall, Ryan Shaw, Tatum Thies

Introduction

* *

*"You know, the SAT dropping the analogy portion
of the test is like Yogi Bear dropping, uh, uh,
something very relatable to a similar thing."*
—Dennis Miller

As comedian Dennis Miller reminds us, the folks at the College
Board have ended the analogy portion of the SAT. Critics
claimed the analogies favored students with larger vocabularies and did little to measure actual reasoning ability. In a public
relations ploy worthy of researchers who, according to New York
Senate testimony, "sit around all day playing with their psychome-
tric navels," the College Board (which owns the test) announced
that the revised SAT provides a stronger link between what students
are taught in school and what they are tested on.

Question: The SAT is now a better indicator of a student's academic potential because

    A. The test eliminates the correlation between affluence
       and high scores.
    B. The test encourages less formulaic writing and more
       original thinking.
    C. Trained readers score the writing samples.

The correct answer is none of the above.

The most significant addition to the "new improved" SAT is the
writing test. More than two million students must face this addi-

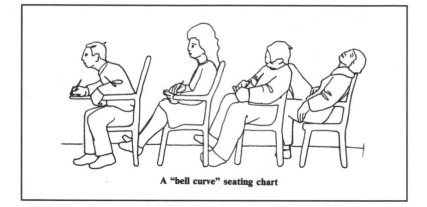

A "bell curve" seating chart

tion, this rite of passage, each year. You, for example. Is this a fair measure of your potential? Hmm ... As a high school student, University of Chicago professor Austan Goolsbee wrote that the SAT should have one judging criterion: "It should be more than a meaningless rite. It should be educationally right."

Goolsbee was on to something. Teachers of writing must battle bravely against the Beast from the East. But how? Peggy Hill, on the animated television show "King of the Hill," echoed the battle cry of most contemporary writing teachers: "You do not come into my house and correct my grammar unless your name is Strunk or White."

Clearly, the classic *Elements of Style* is more revered than any book of its kind. And you could do far worse than worshipping this "geriatric" text. The book you are reading never strays far from the teachings of William Strunk Jr. and E. B. White. After all, the person who reads your essay will reward the clear and correct writing prescribed in *Elements*.

The truth is, lively writing comes from more than simply following the rules. White himself admitted to writing by ear. He knew that expressiveness is not always about exactness. It is more often about taking risks. O frabjous day.

In the *New Yorker*, Adam Lehner spoofed the advice of Strunk and White.

Blessed are the verbose in spirit, for theirs shall be the kingdom of clarity; the inheritance of the ability to name those children who sat beside them in third grade, and of the ability to name many animals, in a singular minute, is what's coming to those who use complicated grammar.

Once again truth trumps fiction. In a 1982 study, Hunter Breland and Robert Jones of the Educational Testing Service (ETS) found that "verbosity" was more important in achieving high scores than such other essay characteristics as "sentence logic," "supporting materials," and "precision of diction." David Owen, who discusses this research in his book *None of the Above*, suggests that test takers should also remember to indent. Evidently, the ETS readers like lots of paragraphs, too.

Of course, much time has passed since the Breland and Jones study. Changes have been implemented. The College Board assures students that these essays will be graded by experienced high school and college English teachers. In an unprecedented experiment to prove that two wrongs can make a right, each essay will be evaluated by two readers, who then will have their scores added together to arrive at your subscore. If the two readers' scores are more than one point apart, a third reader will be called in. Thorough? Yes. Expensive? Oh boy.

In a cover story for *Time*, reporter John Cloud concluded, "The pressure to read fast—and to reward competent but formulaic essays—will be massive." Jane Mallison, a reader of standardized test essays for more than twenty years, compared the scoring of the essays to judging beef stew at the county fair. She said:

You're not grading the beef. You're not grading the sauce. You're not grading the herbs. You're grading the whole stew.

This book, then, is about the stew, the whole stew, and nothing but the stew.

Making This Book Work for You

W e didn't exaggerate. You can significantly improve your chances for a higher score on the SAT by studying this book for three minutes a day. OK, we exaggerated slightly. Conscientious students (and slow readers) may want to invest a few more minutes each day. Practice and review. Practice and review.

In fact, Dr. Tom Fischgrund, author of *Perfect 1600 Score: The Seven Secrets of Acing the SAT*, argues that you "can't overemphasize the importance of SAT review." His study of students who do well on the SAT concluded that scores depend more on preparation than on brains or pure luck.

If that sounds a little too time-consuming for you, remember what celebrity Jennifer Lopez said when asked what she got on the SAT. JLo replied, "nail polish." Apocryphal story or not, just think of what JLo might have accomplished if only she had studied.

To paraphrase Lewis Carroll, they are called lessons because they lessen from day to day. The lessons are explained next. Pay attention. A good manicurist is hard to find. And costly.

The Basic Approach
The Eight-Week, Three-Minute-a-Day Plan

Day 1:   Study the "Introduction" and "Making This Book Work for You" sections.

Days 2–31: Study one writing principle each day. These principles will help you to answer the multiple-choice questions as well as help you to prepare to write the essay. Then, three times throughout the day, review—in your head—the essential ideas taught in that day's principle. The next morning—in the shower—say aloud those same essential ideas. Repeat. And not just the shampoo. Lather too.

Days 32–41: Begin mastering the test strategies. Use the same daily routine that you practiced with the writing principles—one strategy each day.

Days 42–53: Read one practice essay example each day. Study the comments of the grader. Think carefully about the insights provided for each essay.

Days 54–56: Spend one more day on each of the three best essays. Brainstorm different ways that you could implement the characteristics of those essays in the development of various topics.

Day 57: Celebrate. Take as long as you like.

The Advanced Approach

Even a student lost in the bewilderness of the SAT can figure out that the Basic Approach—small masterpiece that it is—falls short of what is really needed. To adequately prepare for the SAT essay, you have to practice writing. You must apply the writing principles and test strategies by writing your own practice essays—the more the merrier (at least on the day you get your SAT score in the mail).

So what should you do? First, follow the Basic Approach. Now add time for applying what you've learned each day in an actual piece of writing. The piece of writing can be the homework you're already doing or an e-mail to a friend or a polite note to your probation officer. But write with purpose. Tiger Woods doesn't just hit golf balls at the driving range. He practices with every club in his bag. And, more important, he always aims at a specific target.

Tiger's goal is to play with his A game. What about you? What is your goal? And that concludes your first *lessen.*

The Last-Minute Approach … or SAT-CPR

You've procrastinated. The SAT is only a week away. How do you resuscitate your chances for essay success? Our prescription: choose one of the following two protocols.

Protocol 1: Skip the writing principles and test strategies sections. Turn to the six practice essay topics. Spend the minutes you've allocated for study on one of the topics each day. Pay special attention to the comments of the grader and to the annotations provided. On the seventh day, rest and review.

Protocol 2: This protocol requires additional time each day but is a more thorough "treatment." Thus, the prognosis for recovery is better. On the first two days, study the writing principles section. On the next two days, study the test strategies section. Work on three of the practice essays for each of the next two days. On the seventh day, rest and review.

What is that word that a doctor shouts when an emergency room patient goes into cardiac arrest? Oh yeah, "clear."

CLEAR!

Good news. You have a pulse. So defibril … later. Study now.

WRITING PRINCIPLES

Three minutes a day is just enough time to brush your teeth, glance over the sports section of the paper, or boot up your computer.

Three minutes a day is also all the time you'll need to learn an important writing principle. In just three minutes (and with a little practice) you can learn why some grammar "truths" are myths, how to cut the clutter out of your writing, and how to make one sentence flow seamlessly into another.

Devote just three minutes a day to each of the principles in this section and you will soon find yourself a more thoughtful and skilled writer. These principles are not just another version of the nearly endless chain of grammar guidebooks. Those books offer a long series of *don'ts*.

Instead, the principles in this section offer lots of *dos*. Do put the most important word at the end of the sentence, do vary the length of your sentences, and do use an occasional metaphor.

So dedicate yourself to a daily three-minute workout. Pump some heavy vocabulary, lift a few semicolons, press a dash, and bench a simile. Easier than a session on the treadmill or stair-climber, these simple, three-minute lessons will bring a new level of fitness to your prose.

The SAT Scars You for Life

Hyperbole. The world's largest ball of string. The world's longest deli sandwich. The world's cranberry capital. We've all heard these claims before. Perhaps your town describes itself as the world's greatest _____ (fill in the blank). No harm done, right? And maybe even a few unsuspecting tourists drop by.

In writing, however, overblown exaggerations quickly erode an SAT reader's faith. Make modest claims. When you write statements that include the words *always*, *every*, or *all*, you make readers grit their teeth. For example, do you feel yourself silently thinking, "Yeah, right" when you read the following:

I never procrastinate.

I always eat healthy.

Everyone should study economics.

Remember the story about the boy who cried wolf. Beware the false alarm.

Young writers are often tempted to exaggerate in the one place where modesty and humility are most becoming: the thesis statement. Imagine a student who was assigned to write an essay on the Lewis and Clark expedition and, much to the student's dismay, more specifically, the prairie dog.

Mystified at how to generate more than a sentence or two on the annoying little pest, he or she pumped some hot air into the thesis, hoping, perhaps, to make the essay seem more important:

> *The prairie dog had a huge impact on the Lewis and Clark expedition. The prairie dog was the species that fascinated and impacted the expedition members more than any other animal.*

This thesis statement is far too grand. Why claim the prairie dog was the most important animal? It wasn't a source of food (such as the buffalo) or a source of fear (the grizzly).

The fact is, you don't need to make a huge claim to have a good thesis. Something simpler, such as "The prairie dog was one of many new animal species that fascinated Lewis and other members of the expedition. The way Lewis studied this creature reveals much about his attitudes toward science and nature," would work well. More important, it wouldn't alienate the kind of SAT readers who are going to dig in their heels and say, "Prove it, buster."

Exaggerating is only human. Consider any angler you've ever met. But just as we keep our skepticism when it comes to fish stories, we are usually alert for any claim that asks too much.

If you want to be believed, go easy on the hyperbole. Those tiny white lies may seem harmless to you, but readers don't like having their legs pulled.

Debunking Grammar Myths

Grammar myths sometimes get in the way of graceful prose. The laws of grammar come and go. We make up rules when we need them and throw them away when we don't.

We've all heard, for example, that we should never use contractions such as *don't* or *won't* in formal writing. Poppycock! Contractions can be both graceful and conversational. We should use them whenever they sound better than writing out the words.

Here are three other common but flawed assumptions that should no longer stifle your writing.

1. **Incomplete sentences are incorrect.** Writers often use incomplete sentences. According to Richard Lederer, author of *Anguished English*, many professional writers begin up to one-tenth of their sentences with conjunctions such as *and* and *but*. Your concern, therefore, should not be with incomplete sentences but with incomplete thoughts.

    In the hands of skillful writers, sentence fragments can perk up prose, making it less stiff and formal. They can also create a nice dynamic with long sentences. Call it, in author Constance Hale's phrase, "pause and effect." For example:

    > *"Man is the only animal that blushes. Or needs to."*
    > —Mark Twain

    Over the years, some English teachers have enforced the notion that *and* and *but* should be used to join elements within a sentence, not to join one sentence with another. Not so. It has been common practice to begin sentences with them since at least as far back as the tenth century. But don't overdo it or your writing will sound monotonous.

2. **Sentences should not start with *there*.** Admittedly, this construction means that the reader won't know the subject at first, but to never begin a sentence with *there* is a mistake. *There* is there to set the stage for what is to come. Use too many sentences, however, that start with "There is" or "There are," and your writing loses energy.

3. **Sentences should not end with a preposition.** Here is another bugaboo that English teachers used to get worked up over. Author Patricia T. O'Connor credits an eighteenth-century grammar book for setting the precedent that somehow caught on with the public. Nobody knows why grammarians insist on living in the past. Writers don't.

   Winston Churchill in one of his witty moments remarked, "A preposition is something you should never end a sentence with." If the prime minister of England can do it, so can you. Just remember that breaking the rules can lead to breakthrough prose.

Think About the Reader First

Writers have many different ways of thinking about the people who will read their work. Some imagine an ideal reader—someone who would read with interest and enthusiasm; some imagine a close friend or relative; some even imagine a disagreeable person who would be likely to find fault at every turn. In each case, having an image in mind of a potential reader helps the writer find the right words to use.

Pretend for a moment that your classmates are your audience for something you're going to write. What do you know about them? Can you guess their average age, number of brothers and sisters, favorite hobbies, possessions, interests, and pastimes? How can you describe their attitudes toward school, jobs, popular music, cars, and clothes? What would they be most interested in knowing about you?

Professional writers must often think carefully about the people who are most likely to read what they are writing. Writers take what those readers like and dislike into consideration as they work. The typical SAT reader is probably an experienced English teacher.

When considering that reader, ask yourself these questions:

- Is my choice of subject appropriate?
- Am I giving my reader new information? Anything he or she doesn't know already?
- Is my material too difficult or too easy?
- How can I connect my message with my reader's interests?

Don't talk to the SAT reader as if he or she is a stranger or somehow beneath you. Consider the reader a sympathetic person who is likely to be interested in anything you find interesting.

Most of all, get off to a good start. The first few words you write often determine whether a reader will stick around. Make your first sentence intriguing, perhaps like these:

- Fourth down and inches to go.
- As a scientist, Throckmorton knew that if he were ever to break wind in the echo chamber he would never hear the end of it.
- I want to die peacefully in my sleep like my grandfather . . . not screaming and yelling in terror like the passengers in his car.

Use your first sentence to set up a problem, to present two sides of a conflict, or to pose a question. Make it impossible, in short, for an SAT reader to quit reading.

"I wish you would make up your mind, Mr. Dickens. Was it the best of times or was it the worst of times? It could scarcely have been both."

One Idea per Sentence

English is getting more and more efficient. That's the conclusion someone fishing for trout might draw upon picking up a copy of *The Compleat Angler* in a local bookstore. *The Compleat Angler*, one of the most popular books of 1653 (OK, maybe there weren't many books in 1653), offers lots of useful tips, such as this:

> *Take this for a rule: When you fish for a Trout with a worm, let your line have so much, and not more lead than will fit the stream in which you fish; that is to say, more in a great troublesome stream than in a smaller that is quieter; as near as may be, so much as will sink the bait to the bottom, and keep it still in motion, and not more.*

The author, Sir Izaak Walton, packs several ideas into a single sentence. We can unpack those ideas—and put them into several sentences—to make our communication more efficient and to help make our angler's life a little easier. For example:

> *If you're going trout fishing, make sure the line you use fits the stream. For example, you'll need a heavier line in a deep river with a strong current. Cast your line in such a way that the bait will sink to the bottom. Then keep the bait slightly in motion, in order to attract the fish you hope to catch.*

A reader would likely have a better shot at a rainbow trout with the modern description. That description, by the way, works because the writer has used only one idea per sentence.

It's generally a prudent idea to serve the SAT reader just one thought at a time. Try to complete that thought before launching a new one. Consider this sentence from a student essay:

> *The choices we have in the student cafeteria are wonderful and the kitchen is open at convenient times for everyone unless you have classes in the middle of the day which is uncommon here at Wesleyan since Wesleyan students like to get a head start on the day with early morning classes.*

That sentence may not make you hungry, but it probably will keep you breathless. Here's how this sentence might have been written in a less confusing manner:

> *The cafeteria offers students a wide choice of times to eat. Early dining hours, for example, are especially convenient for students with morning classes. Students who choose to eat in the middle of the day may encounter some crowded lines, but few have conflicts with classes at those hours.*

"I came. I saw. I conquered," wrote Julius Caesar, and so should you. Put your faith in declarative sentences and develop your ideas, no matter how complicated, one step at a time.

Hold It Together

D o you ever find yourself being put on hold? Maybe you're trying to order a new pair of Air Max Hyperspeed Supernova
shoes from a catalog company, or perhaps you're trying to talk
to a busy friend with call waiting. In any event, you find yourself
patiently idling, waiting to complete your thought after being
interrupted.

The same thing can happen to SAT readers when writers persist
in piling word after word between the subject and verb of a sentence. For example:

> *My brother Louis, whom nobody really likes because he is
> immature but has to tag along with us anyway, is going to the
> movie with us tonight.*

Some readers may have to go back to the beginning of the sentence
to remind themselves who or what the subject was.

Strive to put the main character of the sentence (the subject) as
close as possible to the plot (the verb). Nobody's saying that sentences can't be complex and interesting; they can, as long as they're
easy to follow. But we shouldn't have to read a sentence twice to get
it. For example:

> *We shortly after that found out who wanted to go water skiing
> with us.*

Find a way to put the doer (the subject, *we*) closer to what's being
done (the verb, *found out*):

Soon afterward, we found out who wanted to go water skiing with us.

If subjects and verbs drift too far apart, separated by endless intervening clauses, the reader may give up. Therefore, keep subject and verb together so the reader understands the sentence the first time through. In this sentence, "To get to London we, instead of going over, went under the English Channel," the reader's tendency is to ask "What . . . ?" and possibly quit reading.

Instead, by keeping subject and verb near each other, you ask the reader to cope with just one idea at a time. Hence, "To get to London we went under, not over the English Channel."

On the SAT essay, you are under pressure to write quickly and briefly, much like newspaper headline writers who have learned to tuck their subjects and verbs in the same bed:

*Surprised Troops Hail the Chief (*The president makes an unannounced visit to troops in Iraq.*)*

*For Survivor, Scars Fading Inside and Out (*An eleven-year-old survives a car crash.*)*

French Keep Up Love-Hate Relationship with America (France and the United States still share common values.*)*

The moral of this story is to place one call at a time; talk directly to the reader and keep talking until you've completed your message. Think of your reader as an answering machine, not someone to put on hold.

Making Sentences Hold Hands

The tail feathers of a dove lie over one another in a tight, interlocking pattern that keeps the dove warm and waterproof. The idea makes a good technique for keeping your sentences waterproof, too, something that will impress anyone who reads your SAT essay.

The issue here is how to connect one sentence to the next. When young writers get together to discuss their work, they often say something like, "I wish my sentences flowed better." What they often mean is that they wish one sentence led to the next in a seamless way, "dovetailing," in other words.

The simplest way to dovetail is to repeat a word from the first sentence in the second, as in this example:

> *At the Gap, a basic black sweater ran around $44 plus tax.*
> **This sweater** *was made of wool, cotton, and a bit of cashmere.*

A writer can also use a pronoun to refer to a previous sentence:

> *At the Gap, a basic black sweater ran around $44 plus tax.*
> **This sweater** *was made of wool, cotton, and a bit of cashmere.* **It** *had a ribbed neckline, sleeves, and waist.*

Sometimes the pronoun can be made into an adjective that connects with a different subject. That enables the second sentence to head off in a new direction:

*In the play Mrs. Ethel Savage is a former actress who is now very old, very rich, and very spiteful. **Her** husband has passed away, and **her** greedy children are searching for the ten million dollars in bonds that Mrs. Savage has hidden.*

You can dovetail in a richer, more complicated way by referencing a concept, often by restating it in slightly different terms:

*As with many musicians, the rap artist frequently has **something to say**. Rap is usually criticized because of **its message** of violence, sex, drugs, and obscenity.*

When a writer masters dovetailing, the results can be breathtaking. Notice how smoothly the sentences in this description from *The Water Is Wide* by Pat Conroy flow together:

Yamacraw is an island off the South Carolina mainland not far from Savannah, Georgia. The island is fringed with the green, undulating marshes of the southern coast; shrimp boats ply the waters around her and fishermen cast their lines along her bountiful shores. Deer cut through her forests in small silent herds. The great southern oaks stand broodingly on her banks. The island and the waters around her teem with life. There is something eternal and indestructible about the tide-eroded shores and the dark, threatening silences of the swamps in the heart of the island. Yamacraw is beautiful because man has not yet had time to destroy this beauty.

That's waterproof writing at its best.

Save the Last Dance

Imagine you are a track coach and you're trying to put together a relay team. Where do you put your fastest runner? Where do you put the slowest? Most coaches, it turns out, follow a formula that goes something like this:

- Your fastest runner goes last.
- Your second-fastest runner goes first.
- The two in-between runners go, that's right, in between.

The idea behind this strategy has relevance for writing. You want to get off to a good start. You want to interest your readers and attract their attention. But you also want to save your best for the end. You want your writing to have a payoff.

So, suppose you have three examples to use in support of a point you are trying to make. You would be wise to save your best example for last. Use your second-best example first, and place the other one, the so-so example, in the middle. Putting your best example last should help you clinch your argument.

Let's take a look at how this might work at the sentence level. The most powerful position in a sentence is the last word. Any word next to a period reverberates because the period is a stop sign. Readers must pause over the last word before they move on; it lingers in their mind. When that word appears at the end of a paragraph, it gains even greater emphasis because of the white space that follows it.

Take a look at these examples from student papers:

Does Austin save the day or does Dr. Evil prevail?

At times shopping can be fun, entertaining, boring, interesting, and comical, but it is always, in one way or another, expensive.

Only Nelly could sing a song about tennis shoes and have it be a hit.

None of these writers is particularly sophisticated or accomplished, and yet all know instinctively how to put a key word at the end of a sentence. This principle even works to humorous effect in this unfortunately worded business memo:

The change in maternity leave benefits during the past year has led to some confusion on many people's parts.

The principle here is plain: save your best for last. In time, this will begin to come naturally to you as you write, but in the meantime, use this principle for a few quick revisions. Look back over a paper you've written and find several key sentences. Reread those sentences and consider whether a little rearrangement might produce a more powerful expression—simply by putting the most important word at the end. Once you have reviewed papers you've already written, rearranging sentences on the SAT essay will become second nature.

And if this principle makes sense to you, perhaps you can help answer a tough question. A familiar billboard says, "Eat, shop, relax." Is that really the right order?

The Long and the Short of It

" Eight new choir robes are currently needed, due to the addition of several new members and to the deterioration of some older ones."

The preceding sentence appeared in an actual church bulletin—we can only hope that it was the robes that were deteriorating and not some of the older choir members. The sentence illustrates rather graphically a syntactical problem; that is, a problem stemming from faulty word order. The person who wrote that sentence did not understand the relationships words have with one another. The clarity of a writer's message depends heavily upon proper word placement.

Writers do their hardest work at the level of the sentence. Sentences can generally be described as either "loose" or "periodic." A loose sentence is one in which the grammar is both simple and straightforward. "I went walking with Fred today" is a loose sentence. The subject and verb appear early, and with no complication.

The opposite of a loose sentence is one in which the complexity of subject-verb-object is not resolved until the end—hence the name *periodic* (or, just before the *period*). When a sentence begins, a reader knows to look for certain things, notably the subject and main verb. If something happens to delay them, like prepositional phrases or independent clauses, tension results. The reader waits in a state of suspense. Consider this sentence:

Why you hardly ever come to our meetings is what, for a month, I have been wondering.

The main verb does not arrive until the end of the sentence. Beginning with "Why . . . " may make the sentence slightly more difficult for an SAT reader to process, but it is definitely more interesting than this:

I have been wondering about something for a month. You hardly ever come to our meetings. Why?

Loose sentences are especially effective in short, quick bursts. Their low grammatical tension makes them useful in relating technical information, in giving directions, and in convincing someone that an idea is logical. But a steady succession of loose sentences will bore a reader.

Periodic sentences, on the other hand, are the roller coasters of writing. They resemble the pattern of a mind in flux and keep a reader primed for shocks and reversals. Periodic sentences withhold the main idea until the end for maximum dramatic effect. Look at the variety this writer obtains by the use of three different kinds of periodic sentences:

When Al finally did come back to school, he had become so wrapped up in his own ideas that he was as unable to cope with teachers as they were unable to cope with him. Eventually, after telling his English teacher that he wasn't interested in "kindergarten poetry" and his physics teacher that "physics represent zero in relation to psychics—the real science," he was allowed to graduate on the merits of his earlier work—on the condition that he didn't come to school anymore. This, I believe, must be the first recorded honorable discharge from high school.

Actually, the final sentence is almost a loose sentence; the only interruption is the writer's "I believe." The second sentence is the one that demands the reader's full attention. In that sentence the

writer's grammatical core—that subject-verb-object relationship—
is not completed until the second dash.

If you can alternate loose and periodic sentences, you may liven
up a lackluster paragraph. Make your essay conform more closely
to the rhythms of your thought, and you will make your sentences
more intriguing to the SAT reader.

Re-verb-erate

" It is 8–7, one out, and school will never start, rain will never come, sun will warm the back of your neck forever." With those words, former baseball commissioner A. Bartlett Giamatti charmingly described the allure of America's national pastime. Note, especially, the simple verbs he used: "will never start," "will never come," "will warm."

The best writers work in verbs. As grammarian Karen Elizabeth Gordon put it, "The verb is the heartthrob of a sentence." You would do well to pay close attention to the verbs you use, and one great place to look for exciting verbs is the sports section of your daily paper. Consider these verbs taken from the headlines of a single sports section: stifles, battles, tarnishes, turns back, dominates, shocks, spoils, skins, hangs on, benches, catches, dooms, relishes, blasts. Whew! It must have been quite a day on the gridiron.

Verbs add drama to your sentences. Without them, words would simply mill around, waiting for something exciting to happen. With them, a sentence can shake you up.

One way to check the life of your verbs is to make a count of both active and linking verbs. Baseball writer Roger Angell typically uses about eight active verbs to every one linking verb. If you can come close to that 8:1 ratio, consider yourself in good company.

If you have time, go through your essay and circle every linking verb. Then eliminate as many as possible. For example, you could turn "he has a plan to" into "he plans to" or "the team had ten losses" into "the team lost ten."

If you find an interesting verb, the rest of the sentence practically writes itself. The up and down verbs of the following sentence, for example, make for good reading:

Within the last half year, my self-esteem has plummeted as my weight has shot upward.

People often talk, but are they always speaking? Perhaps they're huffing:

"I'm not," Anthony huffs, "I was just making a comment."

Why settle for a verb like *say* when *holler*, *whisper*, and *insinuate* are available? Consider whether your sentences need to be, in Patricia O'Connor phrase, "reverbed." The verb is the hardest worker in a sentence—choose yours with care.

Oops, There It Is

There is no doubt that starting a sentence with *there* puts the writer on a slippery slope. For one thing, *there* is a ghost subject, a stand-in for the real one. Writers who begin with *there* are essentially saying to the SAT reader, "The star isn't available tonight; instead, playing her role will be . . ."

For another thing, *there* doesn't come by itself. Usually, the writer follows *there* with a being verb, such as *is* or *was*. So now the reader finds a sentence without a real subject and without much of a verb either. That's a recipe for dullness. For example:

There was a sense of pride among the soldiers.

Or:

There is comfort in knowing that I helped.

A companion to *there* is *it*, which often fills the same position in a sentence, as in the following:

It was a perfect day for a picnic.

Sounds like a perfect day for a nap.

And yet, as with so much writing advice, the opposite is sometimes true. Literature is full of examples of terrific sentences that begin with *there*. For example:

"There is a tide in the affairs of men, which, taken at the flood, leads on to fortune."
—William Shakespeare

The student writer in the following passage got *it* right, too, largely thanks to parallel construction:

Stanford is a pretty good school. It's got palm trees. It's got volleyball. It's got huge libraries. It's got a particle accelerator. And it's got some Nobel laureates on the faculty. Not bad at all.

The bottom line is this: starting sentences with *there* or *it* is often a sign of a lazy writer. Such a writer has failed to make the subject the true star of the sentence and has probably failed to find anything worthwhile for the subject to do. Check your essay for *theres* and *its*. Do you see any that could be eliminated in favor of more dynamic nouns and verbs?

But, and this is a tricky "but," sometimes starting a sentence with *there* or *it* is just right. Why? It has to do with the rhythm of your sentence. Read the sentence aloud and in context—perhaps a *there* sentence offers just the pacing you need to finish a timed essay.

A Fragment of Your Imagination

Sometimes a short sentence that gets straight to the heart of the matter can bring home a dramatic point. As a student might say, "There is no need to ramble on and on and on and on and on."

The familiar words "I love you" are a great example of getting everything you want said in three short words. This simple sentence stirs up the same emotion (or more) as would a much longer sentence.

Tom Wolfe once said that if a writer wants the reader to think something is absolutely true, the writer should express it in the shortest possible sentence. Trust me.

Notice how effectively this writer uses short sentences for dramatic effect in this story about a college student who spent a semester in South America:

> As if culture, education, and great food weren't enough, here is another approach to get you to study abroad. You could meet your husband.
>
> Señorita Amanda Miller, a Spanish major, studied in Valparaiso, Chile, last year. She studied at the Universidad Catolica de Valparaiso. "I wanted to study abroad to work on my Spanish," Miller said, "but I also wanted to do something I thought I would never do." Mission accomplished.
>
> Miller met her husband-to-be at a salsa club that she and her friends from the university attended every Thursday. Sparks flew immediately.

Each paragraph ends with a brief sentence—one of five words, one of two words, and one of three words. Those short lines give the whole passage a ring of truth, almost as if the writer were dusting her hands off and saying, "That's that." No further questions needed.

Short sentences, that is to say very short sentences, can also be used to create humor, to put a smile on the SAT reader's face. Here is the lament of a student who found himself dumped for a less savory competitor:

> *You wouldn't think it mattered that much, but the fact she cheated on me with Dave hurt even more. She went from me, a well-dressed, very nice guy who gets good grades, to Dave, who smokes and smells, barely passes classes, and has no respect for anyone. That hurts.*

For pith and power, nothing beats the simple sentence. Newspaper writers know this and bank on it, because in journalism, "You get paid by the period." And if short sentences are good, sometimes fragments are even better. Consider, for example, Muhammad Ali's comments just before a fight with George Foreman:

> *"Only last week, I murdered a rock. Injured a stone. Hospitalized a brick. I'm so mean, I make medicine sick."*

You must be thinking, That's not fair. When I write a sentence fragment, I lose points. What's the difference? Some modern grammarians call these fragments "minor sentences" because even though they're grammatically shortened, they make sense. In other words, it's OK to break the rules when you know you're breaking the rules. Of course, breaking too many rules on the SAT essay could get you penalized, so be judicious.

Tested You Will Be

Imagine a spaceship crash-landing in a remote jungle. The pilot climbs out of the ship and discovers a green gnome standing nearby—a gnome named, of course, Yoda.

Yoda: *Away with your weapon! I mean you no harm. I am wondering, why are you here?*
Luke: *I'm looking for someone.*
Yoda: *Looking? Found someone, you have, I would say, hmm?*
Luke: *Right.*
Yoda: *Help you I can. Yes, mmm.*

What kind of gibberish is Yoda speaking? And more important, is it grammatically correct?

As Luke discovers, Yoda is quite astute, and in more ways than one. Yoda is speaking perfectly good English, although it is English of a rather strange sort.

We are used to sentences that follow a standard subject-verb-object order, as in *Peter Piper picked a peck of pickled peppers*. What Yoda does is simply invert this order by placing the verb or object before the subject:

Hard to see, the dark side is.

Use the force you must, young Skywalker!

These sentences aren't backward, exactly, and they actually aren't difficult to understand. But they do intrigue us because they sound so strange.

You can use this effect yourself, even if you aren't good with a light saber. In the following passage the writer creates an ironic description of her cafeteria and uses inverted word order to highlight the place's alleged cleanliness:

The environment is very pleasing as well. The staff is so avid
about keeping the place spick and span that they'll just
vacuum the floor as you are eating. Talk about overachievers.
The silverware is also kept very clean. Only twice have my
friends had a dirty fork.

Reversing standard word order does cause some English teachers to bristle. That's because it frequently leads to passive sentences, a no-no according to most guidebooks. As Strunk and White put it, for example, "The active voice is usually more direct and vigorous than the passive." Good advice. In most cases, it's a smart strategy to put the subject first.

Passive sentences typically conceal a key piece of information: the subject, or in other words, the responsible party. If you're trying to avoid blame, a passive's your game: "Mistakes were made" or "The pedestrian went under my car."

So it's best not to use passive verbs. But on occasion, it's refreshing to use inverted word order. Tennyson certainly did in his famous poem "The Charge of the Light Brigade": "All in the valley of Death/Rode the six hundred." If you're saving a surprise for the end, here's one more trick hold up your sleeve you should.

Make Pronouns Point

"**W**ho's on first. What's on second. I don't know's on third." These lines from a famous comic routine highlight a common writing error: ambiguous reference. In the routine Bud Abbott and his partner Lou Costello attempt to name the players on a baseball team. Abbott warns Costello that the players have odd names, but this doesn't prevent confusion.

The first baseman's name, for example, is Who. "Who is playing first?" asks Costello. "That's right," replies Abbott. "When the first baseman gets paid, who gets the money?" asks Costello. "Why not?" responds Abbott. "He earned it." And hilarity ensues.

This error plagues almost all writers from time to time, but the development of a critical awareness as you write can help reduce it to the bare minimum. Consider the following sentence:

Garry first became acquainted with Marc one year ago when he enrolled in the lecture and laboratory sections of his molecular biology course.

Who is teaching whom? Was Garry or Marc the student? Pronouns serve as proxies for other nouns. As Patricia O'Connor explains, "Pronouns stand in when nouns don't want to hang around sounding repetitive." But a pronoun should be used only when its reference is clear. The sentence could be improved by substituting either name for *he*. For example:

> *Garry first became acquainted with Marc one year ago when*
> *Marc enrolled in the lecture and laboratory sections of his*
> *molecular biology course.*

Identifying one of the people as a professor, *Professor Duncan* instead of *Garry*, for example, might help too.

This kind of mistake can occur just as easily with plural pronouns:

> *To be sure that her children saw her notes, Mother stuck them*
> *under the magnet on the refrigerator.*

Pronouns are supposed to refer to the most recent noun—*notes*, in this case—but we tend to think *them* refers to people and thus are likely to conclude that Mother stuck her children to the refrigerator. This is a case of referential ambiguity; we don't know which noun *them* is replacing. An improved sentence might look like this:

> *To be sure her children got the message, Mother placed her*
> *notes under the magnet on the refrigerator.*

A pronoun works best when it refers to a specific noun. When the writer asks the pronoun to refer to ideas, things can get murky. For instance:

> *The Missouri River contained many rapids that were located*
> *in the upper portion of the river.* ***This** is when a large boulder*
> *is in the middle of the river and the water runs into the rock,*
> *creating a fast movement.*

Is the word *this* referring to the river, the rapids, the location of the rapids, or even the idea that the river contained some rapids? The answer is unknown, perhaps even to the writer.

Ambiguous pronoun references can also create unintended humor, as in this quote from a church bulletin:

> *Next Sunday a special collection will be taken to defray the cost of the new carpet. All those wishing to do something on the carpet should come forward and do so.*

And doing something takes on new meaning.

All the World's Offstage

Writing is ultimately about reading. Your aim as a writer is to make the SAT reader's job as easy as possible. One way to accomplish that goal is to move yourself out of the way. If you keep intruding between the reader and subject by making yourself the center of the writing universe, you're making life difficult for the reader. As kids might say when someone walks in front of the television, "You make a better door than a window."

Of course SAT readers want to know what happened to you and what you think about things. But you can convey that information without making every other word *me*, *myself*, or *I*. As best you can, try to eliminate phrases like "I think that," or "I believe," or "in my opinion." To anyone reading your essay, it will be clear that these are your thoughts, your opinions, your beliefs. The reader does not need to be continually reminded.

For example, consider this sentence:

I came to college to get a job, and this class did nothing to help me with that.

The sentence raises several questions in the reader's mind: Was the student in the right college? The right class? These questions involve the writer's credibility. To avoid all that and get the reader to the point you want to make, pull *I* and *me* out of the sentence:

This particular class will not help students prepare for a career.

Nothing's been lost and much has been gained.

Sometimes removing yourself from your writing can help you avoid blame—a good thing to remember as you write your SAT essay. Imagine you made this statement to a police officer:

> *The guy was all over the road; I had to swerve a number of times before I hit him.*

Your insurance agent might have counseled you, instead, to say:

> *The guy was swerving so much he was impossible to avoid.*

Now the burden of proof has changed hands. Consider this example from a movie review:

> *Like I said, to make a movie series and have it be good, the plot line should be fairly similar, but new characters, new problems, different settings should all be used.*

The *like I said* phrase leaves the door open for the SAT reader to dismiss the whole argument by thinking, "Well, that's just his opinion." You could achieve a much more authoritative (and believable) tone by leaving out the personal references:

> *For a movie series to be successful, the producers need to add new characters, problems, and settings while continuing a familiar plot.*

But don't fret. Even if you remove *I, me,* and *mine* from your writing, the SAT readers will still love you.

Gender Bender

Remember terms like *repairman, housewife,* and *Mother Nature*? How about phrases such as *act like a lady* and *man to man*? Fortunately, those words have been dumped in the dustbin of history because we have all become sensitized to sexist language.

Instead, we've learned to say (and write) *flight attendant* for *stewardess, handmade* for *manmade,* and even *fair play* for *sportsmanship.* Despite the efforts of some enthusiasts, however, we've resisted *herstory* for *history, spinster of arts degree* for *bachelor of arts degree,* and *male nurse.*

But alas, writers have discovered that it can be more difficult to eliminate sexism when it comes to pronouns. The traditional all-purpose pronoun, for instance, is male. In other words, it's technically correct to write "Each person has his own umbrella" even when each person isn't a him. Sometimes referred to as the "generic he," this pesky pronoun is routinely used when the antecedent noun is singular:

If a student studies hard, he will succeed on the SAT essay.

The way to find a less gender-specific alternative has been fraught with silliness. In an effort to be inclusive, some writers have resorted to the slash as in *he/she* or *he or she*:

If a student studies hard, he or she will succeed on the SAT essay.

That solution works reasonably well in a short sentence but quickly becomes ridiculous when the pronoun must be used repeatedly:

If a student studies his or her geometry and his or her social studies, he or she will likely make the honor roll.

Another popular alternative matches a plural pronoun with a singular noun:

Does each student have their book?

This choice is clearly ungrammatical. Even the best of intentions can't cover a logical mistake like that.

Some writers have decided to alternate using *he* with *she*:

The average student is worried about his grades. Ask the student to turn in her work as soon as possible.

But it's hard to remember whose turn it is, and besides, that hasn't really solved the problem. A few writers have even chosen to always use female pronouns as a sort of grammatical affirmative action. But that just replaces male sexism with female sexism.

Fortunately, there are some better choices. Here are some recommended by the National Council of Teachers of English.

1. **Drop the pronoun altogether.** Instead of "The average student is worried about his grades," use "The average student is worried about grades."
2. **Rewrite the sentence in the passive voice.** Instead of "Each student should hand in his paper promptly," use "Papers should be handed in promptly."

But most of the time, there's an even better solution. Simply make the singular noun plural. Instead of "Give the student his grade right away," use "Give the students their grades right away." Working to eliminate the sexism from your language may seem like too much political correctness, but what's wrong with being fair? It's much harder to overcome a bad impression once you've created one.

Just ask the SAT readerman.

Don't Misunderestimate the Right Place

Sometimes the right word is a new word. Hundreds of words enter our language every year. For example, the Internet has brought us *interface* (to meet, as in "Let's interface"), *multitask* (to do several things at once), and *reboot* (to start over). Slang, especially teenage slang, brings us other words, such as *hottie*, *tight*, *phat*, and *for schizzle* (Snoop Dogg's version of "for sure").

New word combinations also enrich our vocabularies. Recent additions in this category include *suicide bomber*, *weapons of mass destruction*, and *homeland security*. Poets are famous for coining new words. For example, e. e. cummings reminded us that in spring, the world is *mudluscious* and *puddle-wonderful*.

President George W. Bush, or "Dubya" (another new word), has contributed several new words to the national vocabulary, including the oddly logical *misunderestimate*. Paul Payack, chairman of an online dictionary, said, "There are already 11,000 instances of 'misunderestimate' on the Web. The more people use words, the more likely they are to enter the language and last for generations."

Other so-called Bushisms include *embetter* (to make emotionally better—the opposite of embitter), *resignate* (as in, "They said this issue wouldn't resignate with the people"), and *foreign-handed* (as in, "I have a foreign-handed foreign policy").

So, the moral of this story is that it's occasionally OK (*OK*, by the way, is the planet's most frequently used word, no matter what language) to coin words, that is, to make them up. In fact, we do this all the time. It's one of the beauties of our language. If, for example, your group is complaining instead of brainstorming for solutions, you might write that they were *blamestorming*.

On the SAT essay, you're better off sticking to the tried and true. If you do happen upon a clever new word, however, one that just fits your essay, use it with a touch of humility and a good dose of humor. Be sure it's clear that you know the word is a bit off. Otherwise, the SAT rater may just make your new term *misappear*.

Pound the Concrete

ord choice matters, not only on the SAT but for the rest of your life. In fact, choosing the right word on a résumé can make the difference in getting the job you want. Your future employer is looking for the most qualified person to hire. You must rely on words to explain why you are that person. If you select words that are almost right, then you may find yourself almost hired. As Mark Twain once explained, "The difference between the right word and the almost right word is the difference between lightning and lightning bug."

The key is not to generalize in your writing but to use concrete details. General is boring. It asks the reader to stop reading and guess what you mean. Consider the following examples:

general: *worker*   concrete: *assistant manager*
general: *restaurant*   concrete: *International House of Pancakes*
general: *food*   concrete: *strawberry waffles*

Clearly, specific nouns (*salad bar, apron, Mavis*) provide a more detailed picture for the reader. Simply writing that you had a job at a restaurant is vague and uninteresting. You must supply the missing information if you want your writing to be memorable. And this is true in everything you write—your SAT essay, for example.

Comedian Bill Cosby took Shakespeare's famous "Seven Ages of Man" passage and updated it. You'll note that Cosby, too, uses concrete details to make his writing memorable.

*The seven ages of man have become preschool, Pepsi
generation, baby boomer, midlifer, empty nester, senior
citizen, and organ donor.*

If you want to get your prose up and running, keep your abstraction detector in good working order as you write. Be alert for those fuzzy, general, abstract subjects that seem to come to mind when you start a sentence. Suppose, for example, you wanted to analyze movie idol Johnny Depp. The first sentence you think of turns out like this:

*His ability to absorb himself completely in his roles truly gives
an example of pure talent in acting.*

Abstract nouns such as *ability, example,* and *talent* make the whole sentence vague and almost meaningless. What if you had used vivid, specific nouns instead, like this:

*Depp wears thick eyeliner, gold teeth, and matted, nasty hair
to bring his character, pirate Jack Sparrow, to life.*

Those concrete, specific nouns—*eyeliner, teeth,* and *hair*—anchor this sentence in reality and make reading the sentence fun. Of course, if you had Johnny Depp's dimples, you might be reading a Hollywood script right now instead of this book.

Gobble Gobbledygook

Good writers communicate in lean, clean language. They don't waste the SAT reader's time with superfluous words. Just as athletes need strong muscles and low body fat to move quickly and avoid tiring, writers need strong verbs and low writing fat (unneeded words) to set a brisk pace and avoid exhausting the reader.

The following is a flabby memo sent to President Franklin Roosevelt for his approval during World War II:

In the unlikely event of an attack by an invader of a foreign nature, such preparation shall be made as will completely obscure all Federal buildings and non-Federal buildings occupied by the Federal government during an air raid for any period of time from visibility by reason of internal or external illumination.

Here's how Roosevelt trimmed that memo:

If there's an air raid, put something across the windows and turn off the outside lights in buildings where we have to keep the work going.

The memo sent to Roosevelt was couched in gobbledygook—wordy, redundant, unnecessarily complex writing—the antithesis of clear, direct writing. Those who write gobbledygook care more about impressing than communicating.

While such writing might impress those afflicted with Academic Dysfunctional Communication Syndrome, it is a bane to others. Look carefully at your writing to see if every word is carrying its weight. How many words, for example, are really needed in the following sentence? "The Lewis and Clark expedition was thought up by the president of the United States of America; at that time it was Thomas Jefferson." Would "The Lewis and Clark expedition was conceived by President Thomas Jefferson" get the job done just as well?

To be technical, don't let adjectives and adverbs weaken your message. Be on the lookout for useless adjectives, as in these examples, with corrections in parentheses: *past history* (*history*), *personal opinion* (*opinion*), *baby kitten* (*kitten*), and *blue in color* (*blue*).

In the same way, watch for places where you can use a strong verb to replace a weak adverb. Here are some examples:

Instead of	*He **ran quickly** down the field.*
Prefer	*He **sped** down the field.*
Instead of	*The cat **suddenly jumped** on the mouse.*
Prefer	*The cat **pounced** on the mouse.*

Or: *The student sped down the hallway and pounced on the SAT.* You get the idea.

Some Words are Very, Very Bad

It seems odd, doesn't it? Your mother probably told you that certain words should *never* be used in polite company. You know the words. Yes, *those* words. And yet there are certain words that we commonly use when we talk but should never use in print. How can that be?

These unmentionable words are vague qualifiers, words such as *really*, *very*, *truly*, *basically*, and *totally*. They are valuable in speech because they allow us to buy a little breathing time—we can get by with the less-than-precise word until we have time to think of what we mean to say exactly.

But when we write, we can be more selective. When we use fewer qualifiers, our sentences become tighter, clearer, and more concrete. Thus, *very happy*, or worse, *very, very happy* becomes *joyful*.

For example, notice the qualifiers this writer uses in a description of a wedding reception:

The food was very good and tasty. It was a buffet, which included fruit, roast beef, baked potatoes, turkey, and rolls. The turkey and potatoes were a little cold, but overall it was very good. The dance was very fun, and a lot of good songs were played. The dance floor was filled with many people having fun and dancing like fools. Overall, the whole experience was very elegant. The wedding was a little longer than usual but was very beautiful. The dinner and dance were also held at a very nice place with great food and a fun dance.

You might think this example is silly, but consider whether vague qualifiers such as *very* sneak into your prose without your ever noticing. Remove the qualifiers, sharpen a few observations, and you might get this:

> *The wedding reception featured a tasty buffet with fruit, roast beef, baked potatoes, turkey, and rolls, though some of the food was cold. After dinner, the dance floor began to fill with people making fools of themselves—an especially amusing sight because everything else about the event was elegant. The wedding may have taken longer than usual, but the location, the buffet dinner, and the dance all made for an enjoyable evening.*

Is this a universal rule, something true in every case? No. In the hands of great writers, anything is possible. All the rules go out the window. Here Stephen King uses *really* in a most effective way:

> *Of course movies matter. But, you might ask, do movies **really** matter? Do they matter the way great books do, or great plays like* King Lear? . . . *My answer is you bet your sweet round fanny.*

Still, if you can strip the qualifiers from your sentences most of the time, you'll get your writing down to where the rubber hits the road. Then you can let nouns and verbs do the heavy lifting as in this student evaluation: "This class made me laugh, sometimes cry, dry my eyes to try and try, question reality, laugh at authority, scoff at accepted truths, and made me long to teach poetry."

And I Said What I Meant

The main object of prose writing is the transfer of meaning from writer to reader—clearly, and in the fewest words possible. Striving to write efficiently can help you cope with the time constraints posed by the SAT essay.

Simple and direct language, and generally short sentences and paragraphs, make the SAT reader's job easier. Don't force readers to use their mental energy wrestling with unnecessarily difficult or cloudy writing. Let them save that energy for complex ideas.

Writing that is choked with polysyllabic words, for example, can make hard reading. Have you ever read a product manual, article, or textbook that was so foggy that you had to work just to tease the meaning from one paragraph? Who hasn't, right?

But wait, you say, that was a complex subject, and a complex subject needs complex language. Wrong. Just because you're dealing with a complicated subject doesn't mean your language has to be.

W. Somerset Maugham put it this way:

I have never had much patience with the writers who claim from the reader an effort to understand their meaning. You have only to go to the great philosophers to see that it is possible to express with lucidity the most subtle reflections. You may find it difficult to understand the thought of Hume, and if you have no philosophical training, its implications will doubtless escape you; but no one with any education at all can fail to understand exactly what the meaning of each sentence is.

That said, it's also true that complex words and sentences are needed in good writing, but the point is to find the right balance between high-octane writing (rich, polysyllabic words and phrases) and more economical, utilitarian prose (single-syllable words).

Monitor your writing. Select 100 consecutive words from a practice essay and divide by the number of sentences. The result will give you your average sentence length. Studies have shown that an average of 16 or 17 words fits most readers' comfort level.

It takes skill and an ordered mind to express complex ideas in simple language. Remember Albert Einstein's $E = mc^2$? The more complex the idea, the greater the need to keep your language simple.

Cut the Clutter

eyewitness at the scene

10:00 A.M. in the morning

two twins

I f you can't see an easy way to shorten those phrases without los-
ing the meaning, you may be guilty of repetitiveness in your
writing. It's an easy trap for all of us.

The fact is, though, good writing is efficient. An ethical writer
shouldn't ask any more of the SAT reader's time than is strictly necessary. And when you repeat yourself, you're asking more from the
reader than you're entitled to. So the challenge is to be on guard
lest redundancies slip into your sentences unnoticed.

One of the easiest ways to be redundant is to add a useless preposition at the end of a phrase: *canceled **out**, went **away**, shouted **out**,
send **in**, continue **on**.* The prepositions *up* and *down* are especially
dangerous—*open **up**, wrote **down**, fell **down**, divided **up**,* and so on.

Another form of repetition occurs when a writer puts a synonym
on either side of *and*—for example, *safe and sound, plain and simple, each and every.* We also use two words where one would get the
job done. See if you can reduce each of the following by one or two
words:

absolutely necessary
advance planning
ask the question

at the present time
basic fundamentals
close proximity
other alternatives
refer back
both of them
in the year 2004
first of all

Sometimes you can think of a different word to replace a string of words:

on one occasion . . . . .once
a small number of . . . . .a few
went on to say . . . . .continued
all of a sudden . . . . .suddenly
a large number of . . . . .many
was able to make his escape . . . .escaped

With a little work and some careful editing, you can do your part to slim down American prose. Here's how. Take this passage of thirty-six words:

Weight loss is a constant battle in which it seems there is no end. A friend of mine recently told me that she used to have an eating disorder and continues to struggle with it currently.

And cut it in half:

Weight loss is a constant battle. A friend recently told me she is still struggling with an eating disorder.

Sometimes a loss is a gain.

An Element of Stylin'

$\int$ tyle in writing refers to the voice readers hear speaking to them between the lines. Voice, as you might guess, implies personality. What kind of person does your SAT reader think you are? How does the reader form that impression?

When a writer selects a style, however unconsciously, and thus presents a personality to a reader, in Walker Gibson's words, he or she "chooses certain words and not others, and prefers certain arrangements of words to other possible arrangements." Every choice you make is significant to style.

Let's take a look at three familiar styles in modern American prose—Tough Talk, Sweet Talk, and Stuffy Talk. The way we write at any given moment can be a form of one of these three basic styles, or perhaps a combination.

Tough Talkers are mainly concerned with themselves—their style is I-talk. Sweet Talkers go out of their way to be nice to us—their style is you-talk. Stuffy Talkers express no concern for themselves or their reader—their style is it-talk. Tough Talkers tend to use a lot of one-syllable words, while Stuffy Talkers prefer two- or three-syllable words. Sweet Talkers are somewhere in between.

Here's an example of Tough Talk by one of the toughest talkers of all time, Ernest Hemingway:

> In the late summer of that year we lived in a house in a village that looked across the river and the plain to the mountains. In the bed of the river there were pebbles and boulders, dry and white in the sun, and the water was clear and swiftly moving and blue in the channels.

Here's some Sweet Talk from the world of advertising:

You may have tried Kraft Dinners before and been delighted at how quick and easy they are—and how unusually good. Well, wait till you taste these new Dinners from Kraft. They're complete, the finest of their kind, made with all the best Kraft ingredients.

And a little Stuffy Talk from government bureaucrats:

In previous studies the use of tobacco, especially cigarette smoking, has been causally linked to several diseases. These widely reported findings, which have been the cause of much public concern over the past decade, have been accepted in many countries by official health agencies, medical associations, and voluntary health organizations.

To determine your own style, take a short chunk of your writing and count the words. If three-fourths (75 percent) or more of the words you use are one-syllable words, you're a Tough Talker. Sweet Talkers use about two-thirds and Stuffy Talkers about half. Now count the number of words with more than two syllables. If the percentage is low (about 5 percent), you're a Tough Talker. Stuffy Talkers use about 25 percent. As you might guess, the Tough Talker mainly writes in first person (*I, me, mine*), the Sweet Talker in second person (*you, your*), and the Stuffy Talker in third person (*he, she, they*).

The goal is to adjust your style for the particular writing task you face. If you're writing an e-mail message to a friend, Tough Talk works just fine. If you're trying to convince Mom or Dad to pay for your car insurance, try Sweet Talk. If you're writing a research paper on T. S. Eliot, Stuffy Talk might be the best choice. On the SAT essay, a combination of Tough and Stuffy is probably best. Save the Sweet Talk for those warm, romantic moments *after* the test.

The Rolling Tones in Concert

Tone might be described as the emotional quality a writer brings to the work. We expect a dark painting to be somber, perhaps even mysterious. Words can command the same effect: no one would mistake Poe's macabre tone in a poem or story.

The following example, written as a description of a Rolling Stones concert, certainly conveys an emotional tone:

> *Being July Fourth, it was mighty hot, and believe me everyone dressed for the occasion. There was an influx of hot pants, halter tops, one-size-fits-all bras, and, last but not least, one birthday suit that was soon to have the candles blown out.*

This writer reveals a sense of excitement, but just exactly what caused that excitement is hard to know. This is tone in search of meaning.

By contrast, sometimes language is almost atonal, that is, without any emotional coloring at all. The various publications of the government are examples of the purest objective writing. In those official reports, emotional connotations are played down as much as possible.

The following example was written not by a government bureaucrat but by a student who was probably trying too hard to please. Her writing might be termed "overcontrolled." The descriptions are precise, but they have the effect of dehumanizing her characters.

> *The presence of older people at Northern Virginia Community College is a tremendous asset to the educational opportunities it offers. Their influence upon the people around them is obvious. They are a stabilizing force in a changing community, and they have the capacity to slow us down, to make us think. We respect them, and we learn from their vast sources of experience. Perhaps most important, these special individuals lend a certain degree of reality to classroom situations.*

This kind of writing sounds like something a machine might have composed. A better balance between these two extremes—all emotion and no emotion—is needed.

One way a writer can prove an ability to control a word's emotional impact as well as its literal meaning is by using irony. In the following example, a writer proposes a change that will revolutionize human life, but his tone resembles that of a city council ordinance.

> *While I am not advocating complete removal of the law of gravity (Lord knows where we would be without it), there is no doubt in my mind that a great majority of the population would benefit from the elimination of this "Mickey Mouse" law. Under my plan, the force of gravity would be minimized in areas where it has the greatest detrimental effect; i.e., near the ground or in sections of water beneath famous bridges such as the Brooklyn or Golden Gate bridges.*

The moral of this story is that a writer should be sensitive to the emotional nuances of words. Now, where's Mick Jagger when we need him?

Seeing with Your Ears

"**A** good word is worth a thousand pictures," said Eric Sevareid, a longtime CBS radio and television correspondent. Sevareid understood the power of words to influence our thinking. When we hear words on the radio—without the benefit of seeing what is described—we create the pictures in our minds. "TV gives everyone a picture," Peggy Noonan, speechwriter for President Ronald Reagan, said, "but radio gives birth to a million pictures in a million minds."

Now you may never become a presidential speechwriter, but you do want the SAT reader to remember what you say and to take your ideas seriously. To make those ideas memorable, put a picture in the reader's mind.

Take Shakespeare, for example. We can't forget these words: "Friends, Romans, countrymen, lend me your ears." As comic Bob Newhart wondered, would anyone have paid attention to, "Listen up, folks. I've got something I want to tell you."

One way to give your readers some mental images is to use similes or metaphors. These eccentric and sometimes outrageous comparisons join two unlike things. For example:

I felt as if I were drowning in homework.

Or:

Then he kissed her, like a butterfly kisses the windshield of a Porsche on the autobahn.

A simile uses the words *like* or *as* to help make the comparison, as in the following examples:

She yelled at us like a cheetah tearing into flesh.

Or:

Words rolled through the air from my teacher's mouth like a tumbleweed rolling across the desert of my brain.

It's not hard to imagine a wild animal eating or a tumbleweed blowing across a desert. Mental images similar to these can pop into the head of the reader, who then thinks, "OK, yeah, now I know what you're talking about."

Metaphors, on the other hand, are direct comparisons and need no other help: "I feel the chains of stress and monotony weighing down on my weary spirit." By using two things that are seemingly unrelated (stress and chains), the writer gives us a sense of how drastic or serious the situation might be. Chains, as we know, are heavy and tiresome; by applying them to stress, we get a sense of what turmoil the narrator is going through.

Metaphors are a challenge because they must be original, created expressly for a particular time and place. A metaphor lasts about as long as chicken left out on the counter—use it while it's fresh and then forget about it. Once-clever metaphors quickly become worn out and empty.

So, when you're looking to create a memorable image, turn to your old friends simile and metaphor. After all, you are the artist with the word palette.

Making Your Essay Count

The three bears. The three little pigs. Cinderella and her two ugly stepsisters. Three is clearly the magic number when it comes to storytelling. Three is somehow satisfying: not too many, not too few, just right.

Speechwriters often search for three examples of whatever point they wish to make. The first example causes the listener to think, "Oh, I suppose." The second example causes the listener to think, "Well, that seems right." The third example, the clincher, is the one that causes the listener to think, "Why, yes, that must be it." The number three just seems to have an aura of invincibility.

But other numbers have value for writers too. Take one, for example, the "loneliest number" as the rock band Three Dog Night once sang. The number one commits the writer to a single thought: "Make mine a latte." In this simple sentence, as writing coach Roy Peter Clark notes, the writer declares a single defining characteristic. The reader must focus on that and nothing else. For example:

Just do it.

I have a dream.

I have a headache.

The number two has its own special talents. Use it, for example, to complicate issues. "Make mine a latte with a shot of espresso." Here the writer doesn't ask us to make a choice; instead, the writer makes us hold two possibilities in our minds at the same time. For example:

Green eggs and ham

Grits and gravy

Donald Trump and "You're fired"

Sentences with two items ask the reader to balance, to compare and contrast. They place us on the twin horns of a dilemma.

That brings us back to three. The number three enables us to surround a subject, to triangulate, as it were. "Make mine a latte with a shot of espresso and add some whipped cream on top." Now we see the subject in a well-rounded way. In our culture, three seems to give us a sense of the whole. For example:

Beginning, middle, and end

Of the people, by the people, for the people

Larry, Moe, and Curly

At the end of his famous passage on the nature of love in the Book of Corinthians, Paul writes, "For now, faith, hope, and love abide, these three." Could he have said it any better?

So, writing is as easy as one, two, three, right? Well, what about four? Five? Six? Once the writer goes beyond three, the sky's the limit. "Make that a double latte with a shot of espresso, whipped cream, a whisper of cinnamon, and a cocoa bean on the side."

What do more examples add to a sentence—a list, a roster, an inventory? They provide a powerful sense of detail. "The Lewis and Clark expedition encountered the Omaha, Ponca, Arikara, Mandan, Hidatsa, Shoshone, Nez Percé, Clatsop, and Walla Walla tribes, to name a few."

As for the SAT essay, think six. More coffee, anyone?

Too Close to Call

The semicolon is a much-neglected beast. A. P. Rossiter, one of the finest Shakespearean commentators of his generation, was a champion of the semicolon; he rarely let a paragraph go by without finding some reason to slip one in. But many writers, and particularly students, seem to use it with great reluctance. And yet the semicolon offers interesting possibilities to bring variety and elegance to your writing.

The semicolon is useful when two independent thoughts belong together in one sentence. The semicolon connects independent elements; that is, it joins two groups of words that could each stand alone but somehow have something important in common.

With the semicolon, what you see is what you get: it acts like a period and a comma fused. It can be distinguished from its close relative, the colon, by this principle of independence—the words that follow a colon do not need to be able to stand alone. Compare these two sentences:

1. He liked all kinds of vegetables: peas, beans, collards, and potatoes.
2. He liked all kinds of vegetables; he particularly liked peas, beans, collards, and potatoes.

The semicolon can also be used to separate items in a series when those items already use commas, as, for example, in a list of cities:

Pierre, South Dakota; Bismarck, North Dakota; and Ames, Iowa

Or a sentence like this:

> *From a balcony, one can not only hear the gossip about*
> *Signora Benetti's daughter, but one can see Anna*
> *industriously setting the dinner table for her mamma; one*
> *can hear Ricardo's fingers gently meandering over the strings*
> *of his guitar; and one can smell the pasta and sauce which*
> *each good Italian mamma in the neighborhood is preparing*
> *for dinner.*

But this is easy. What really requires the writer's delicacy is to create a sentence with a fragile balance between two separate thoughts that seem to have one common purpose:

> *Fletcher Christian's men, after taking over the Bounty,*
> *seemingly disappeared from the face of the earth; nearly*
> *twenty years were to pass before their hiding place was found.*

Some people say that semicolons are most frequently used in formal language, that professors are fond of them because they make sentences long—and long sentences appear to be more intellectually rigorous. But they work for all of us.

If you find yourself using *and* too often or notice that you've written too many short, choppy sentences, give the semicolon a try. It won't just make your sentences better; it will make them more interesting too—especially to a beleaguered SAT reader.

Add Some Body Language

The showman Victor Borge once had a comic routine in which he gave sounds to punctuation. A comma, said Borge, sounds like a squiggle looks, and he would make a noise roughly equivalent to the sound of a rag cleaning a glass window. A period sounded like the German word for period, *punkt*. And of course, the semicolon was a combination of those two sounds. Borge's colon was a double punkt, and his dash was a vocal rendition of the sound Zorro's sword used to make. Once Borge had demonstrated the sound of each of these marks, he would use them as he read poetry aloud to the audience.

Borge's routine reminds us that the writer makes music in the mind's ear. In particular, two punctuation marks—the dash and the colon—can provide the rhythm of jazz to writing.

For example, Borge's dash (the sword of Zorro) was swift—the dash speeds up a sentence. It signifies an immediate association in the writer's mind between one thing and another and propels the SAT reader furiously from one thought to the next.

Use the dash to indicate a sudden change in tone. For example:

On the mosquito's sides had been two flattened sacs, and from them she now pulled out—wings!

Use the dash when you want to add something by shouting:

The next day Mrs. Blakewell—what a pest she is!—complained to Dad about the noise we had made.

And the dash can be used at the end of a sentence when the writer wishes to make an abrupt point or summary:

We had only one choice—escape.

Meanwhile, let's not forget another useful mark: the colon. Remember that Borge's colon was a double period and hence almost a double stop. It gives the writer a way to tell the reader to hit the brakes but then to continue, sort of like a flashing red light. The colon is helpful for introducing a list:

For a first date, you have a few options: you can go out to eat, you can go to a movie, or you can go to someone's house and watch TV.

Or dramatizing a leap in thought:

Cancer: one of life's biggest threats.

The colon performs many of the same functions as the dash but at a more leisurely pace. When pondering which to use, consider whether your reader is dashing out the door for work or idling in an easy chair, watching the snow fall outside the window.

And if you really want to make an impact, add a few italics, as in this example from Betsy Haynes's teen romance *The Truth About Taffy Sinclair*:

Suddenly I saw something that made my heart stop. Jana Morgan and her friends were standing in a tight little cluster looking at something that Jana was holding. They were giggling and talking excitedly. I knew without looking. They had found the last thing in the world I wanted them to see—*my secret, personal diary!*

Ah yes, the truth and Taffy are sometimes stretched.

Parenthetically Speaking

Most of the pens and pencils I own don't seem to have a volume control. In fact, none of them do. And yet all of them are capable of helping to raise or lower a writer's voice.

You can use parentheses when you want to whisper. In this sentence, for example, "The teacher told me I had a 1.6 GPA (whatever GPA means)," the writer didn't want to announce his or her ignorance to the whole world—at least not very loudly.

Parentheses can be used to add a comment in the middle of a sentence. "One of my idiot friends (idiot being an understatement) did the dumbest thing today." Parentheses are also used to enclose comments directed straight at the reader: "How much is $40 thousand worth to Martha Stewart? That amount of money works out to roughly .006 percent of her net worth (nothing to lose sleep over)."

Parentheses set off material that the author does not consider necessary to understand the basic meaning of the sentence. A remark tucked inside a pair of parentheses looks as if the writer could have dropped it altogether (which is why it was hidden inside parentheses). Sometimes when students read passages aloud, they skip over anything inside parentheses, instinctively recognizing the nonessential.

But parentheses also allow a writer to develop a double voice. They enable the writer to comment on the action, much like a stage manager explaining a play to the audience. Those comments can be ironic:

Class time is (unfortunately) used to maximum potential.

Or humorous:

> *"The Simpsons" remains one of the best programs on television with its priceless Homerisms ("We love queens, be they homecoming or dairy") combined with sight gags and celebrity cameos.*

Or even allow a dog to think:

> *Then he stroked my nose (I tell you, he really does love me!), brushed my fur, adjusted my leash, and pushed me out the door.*

By the way, did you notice the exclamation point? Exclamation points create a powerful contrast to parentheses because they indicate strong emotion, either positive or negative: "Stop, you can't go in there!" or "Henry, I love you!"

When you state something with emotion, you can't really do much to make the reader feel that emotion. Are you going to write it in big bold letters? No. Are you going to underline it? No. That's where exclamation points come in.

Check out how exclamation points affect how you interpret these sentences:

> *"Wait, don't touch that button!"* (You're not asking people politely; you're trying to scare the bejesus out of them.)

> *"Oh Romeo, I love you so much!"* (This isn't a crush in junior high; this is deep down love.)

But use both parentheses and exclamation points sparingly in your SAT essay. They can give the readers a feeling that you are standing over their shoulders and either whispering or shouting in their ears. That can be fun for a while—a short while.

The Pudding Is in the Proof

Imagine that you have just five minutes to finish your SAT essay. You frantically check your progress. Whoops. You haven't thought of a conclusion yet, and you wanted to go back and fix the first sentence. Yikes.

But have you proofread? "Proofread? Yeah, right," you say to yourself. "I barely have time to write another sentence. Why proofread anyway; that's the teacher's job."

Actually, proofreading is an essential step in the writing process. The essay is not complete when you stop writing. Simple spelling errors, such as those that a click on the spell-check button would fix, show the SAT reader that you don't sincerely care about your essay.

Here are a few pointers for proofreading. After you finish your essay, take a moment's break (I know, you'll have to plan ahead). Read once through to check the sense. Even though the sentences are grammatically correct and none of the words are misspelled, something might still be wrong:

Loida Whitson called her sister, Dorcas, in the Philippines on Dorcas's thirtieth birthday. She talked to everyone there. (That might have been quite a phone bill!)

He walked across the room and kissed her where she sat. (I'll bet she was surprised!)

Use common sense, too. Look for places where the meaning could be misconstrued, such as in these church bulletin bloopers:

Our next song is "Angels We Have Heard Get High."

Remember in prayer the many who are sick of our church and community.

Weight Watchers will meet at 7:00 P.M. Please use large double door at the side entrance.

Be on the lookout, too, for words that are slightly askew:

When Christopher Columbus and his European comrades first set foot on North American soil in 1492, it did not take long for them to run into the Native Americans who inhibited the land. (I wonder how the Native Americans lost their inhibitions?)

Finally, try reading your paper aloud (very quietly, of course). Anything that makes you cringe when you hear it needs rewriting.

Proofreading is that little bit of extra time and effort you put into your essay that will take it from ordinary to extraordinary—the breast paper you can write!

Things Are Looking Up

You can't use a dictionary on the SAT essay, but you can use one every other time you write. And you should. A dictionary is a writer's single greatest resource. A thesaurus, stylebook, or writing guide may be helpful at times, but they can never replace the good old dictionary.

Dictionaries supply a writer with a great wealth of material: they provide a word's most common meaning, together with examples of its use; secondary meanings; and some indication of the word's origin—useful information when questions of tone arise. Generally, words of Latin origin are longer and blandly neutral; words of Anglo-Saxon origin are frequently shorter and more vivid. Special dictionaries such as the *Oxford English Dictionary* provide other information including a history of the word's meaning (which can change from age to age).

Writers who have the slightest hesitation about the precise meaning of a word should consult a dictionary. That way, they can avoid problems such as those in the following humorous examples from some course evaluations:

*This class is fun and inciteful. (*There must have been some heated discussions!*)*

*The class has stretched my limitations. (*One of those limitations is writing, apparently.*)*

It's a challenge to read some of the more deviant works. (Not to mention diverse or offbeat.)

A dictionary can also help you avoid trouble like this:

He lets me think anteliticly about the books I am reading. (Let's analyze that.)

My only quam in this class . . . (I wonder whether a quam tastes anything like a clam.)

A dictionary can even help you know whether a word can be used as an adverb:

I have upmost enjoyed this class and having you as a professor.

As a verb:

She listens to our views and inputs her own as well.

Or as an adjective:

She gives clear explanations of terms and if the students are confused, she makes it further clear.

These days the best modern dictionaries even have pictures. Be sure that you have this essential reference work close at hand whenever you sit down to practice writing your SAT essay.

TEST STRATEGIES

"My personal theory is that it has to do with how much money you send them in the mail. I think the amounts they tell you to send are actually just suggested minimum donations—if you get my drift."
—columnist Dave Barry

D espite Barry's cynical theory that the SAT is for sale, you still have a better chance of buying love or a member of Congress. So let's barter. You study the strategies, you get a higher score.

Have a Plan B

"One stupid test and I'm roadkill on the highway of natural selection. Do you realize my entire future is nothing more than a barren expanse of minimum wage jobs and reality TV? All leading to my eventual extinction."
—Warren Cheswick, "Ed"

On one episode of the television show "Ed," high school student Warren Cheswick bemoans his fate after learning of a low score on the SAT. Fortunately, Cheswick has a plan B. The plan, however, is not to study harder and retake the SAT. Cheswick decides, instead, to give up the idea of going to college altogether. Cheswick's plan B is to immediately start his career as a talk show host on public-access television. Dare to dream, his mantra.

You are not a character on a television show. Granted, the "Tonight Show" may be in your future, but not tonight while you're preparing for an essay question. What happens if that question makes no sense to you? Or if you can't think of anything substantive to say?

It's not how much you know that counts but how well you use what you do know.

Consider the following suggestions.

1. Practice on the Nearly Impossible

In J. D. Salinger's *The Catcher in the Rye*, the central character, Holden Caulfield, flunks history. His teacher, Mr. Spencer, informs

Holden that he knew "absolutely nothing." Then Spencer reads Holden's essay exam aloud and forces him to listen.

The Egyptians were an ancient race of Caucasians residing in one of the northern sections of Africa. The latter as we all know is the largest continent in the Eastern Hemisphere. . . .

And so on. You are more fortunate than Holden. You don't have to know any facts about the Egyptians—or much else for that matter. The SAT essay question allows you to merely apply what you already know. The key is to make a meaningful connection between what is asked and what you know. Remember: *works of literature speak to each other.*

Suppose you were given the following essay topic.

Consider carefully the excerpt and the assignment below it. Then plan and write an essay that explains your ideas as persuasively as possible. Keep in mind that the support you provide—both reasons and examples—will help make your view convincing to the reader.

In Mark Twain's book *The Adventures of Huckleberry Finn*, Huck becomes more than a casual rebel against responsibility. His destiny is to learn much about what it means to be a human being. On his journey down the Mississippi, Huck meets up at one point with two ne'er-do-wells: the king and the duke. The duke refers to the people who live along the river with disdain.

". . . these Arkansaw lunkheads couldn't come up to Shakespeare; what they wanted was low comedy—and maybe something ruther worse than low comedy, he reckoned. He said he could size their style."

Assignment: What is your view on the differences that separate people? In an essay, support your position using an example (or examples) from literature, the arts, history, current events, politics, science and technology, or your experience or observations.

Now suppose you haven't read *The Adventures of Huckleberry Finn* (if so, shame on you). You are limited, therefore, to the insights you can glean from the passage quoted. Even if you are unaware that Huck is one of the good bad boys of American literature, you can infer from the passage that Twain favored him over the people of Arkansas. Is Twain's book titled *The Adventures of the Arkansaw Lunkheads*? And you are told in the blurb that the king and the duke are "ne'er-do-wells."

So your plan B becomes to flesh out the essay by applying what you have been studying recently. Let's say that your English class just finished discussing "anyone lived in a pretty how town" by e. e. cummings. At first thought, you might assume Huck and "anyone" had little in common. Don't give up so easily. Study the quoted passage again.

In cummings's poem, the "lunkheads" are the "someones" and "everyones" in life who act dutifully without joy or pleasure. Not really alive, they remain unchanged while "anyone" blossoms. The tragedy, you learn in the cummings poem, is the fate of the children. Raised by the "someones" and "everyones" of the world, these children lose their capacity to grow, in all senses of the word. Huck, you could argue, is "anyone"—a homeless waif who finds his way despite the people who surround him—the people who are already "dying," even as we first encounter them.

Other works of literature will work as well. In Athol Fugard's play *"Master Harold" . . . and the Boys*, the character Sam describes the collisions that take place between people. Using ballroom dancing as a metaphor, Sam explains how easily we are bruised by our differences—how people get hurt by all the bumping. That, as you might suspect, is part of what Huck learns about the nature of human beings.

And don't forget that you can write about your own experiences. Your journey through high school, like Huck's trip down the Mississippi, is a quest for self-knowledge. You, too, have learned much about what separates people. How accepting of a person's differences is your average clique in high school? *Go team!*

Now it's your turn. Try preparing for the SAT by answering some essay questions that are far more difficult than those questions likely to be asked by the College Board. You and a friend should make up practice essay questions for each other. Evaluate each other's completed essays. Discuss. Rethink.

2. Add to Your Tool Chest

Terry Deibel, a National War College strategist, warns, "If the only tool you've got is a hammer, every problem looks like a nail."

Even the most intransigent of desk-perados will benefit from studying the principles, strategies, and practice essays in this book. You need these tools to better prepare for any contingency.

You should also read more. Read the editorial page of a national newspaper. Contemporary poetry. Collections of short stories. Your homework. Feed your brain. Anything and everything. Dr. Tom Fischgrund's study of students who earned perfect SAT scores found that those students read nearly twice as much for school as average academic achievers. Fischgrund concluded, though, that it really didn't matter much *what* was read. The key was to read a lot.

Keep in mind that every book you read becomes a part of you. And you want a committee of writers in your head to serve as editors for your writing. Someone on that committee should be the voice in your head screaming at you when you construct a poorly worded sentence. Another someone should whisper sweet nothings when you occasionally make sense. Collectively, these writers invited into your thinking keep your tools sharpened and at their ready.

3. Seek Sense and Sensibility

Broaden the sphere of people that influence your thinking. Include folks other than the celebrity of the moment or the popular politician. The goal here is to develop an artistic sensibility. Biographer Eric Lax wrote that Woody Allen combines "the cadences of Bob Hope, the language of S. J. Perelman, the style of George Lewis, the outlook of Mort Sahl, the obsessions of Ingmar Bergman, the zaniness of the Marx Brothers, the soulfulness of Buster Keaton, the existential dilemma of Jean-Paul Sartre, the exaggerated exoticness of Federico Fellini . . . to produce a unique sensibility."

Of course, you won't have the same influences as Allen. Nor should you. After all, Allen once admitted that he was obsessed by the fact that his mother genuinely resembled Groucho Marx. But the likelihood of writer's block greatly decreases if you welcome creative people into your neighbor-head.

4. Accept That Life Is Not Always Fair

The *Albuquerque Journal* cites this case of health care contingency planning: Surgeons cut a hole in a man's head to relieve swelling after an accident. The hospital's finance office then refused to schedule a follow-up procedure to replace the piece of skull because it was no longer an emergency.

The man did have a plan B. According to the surgeons, "The man wore a baseball cap to protect his brain until the hospital finally agreed to do the procedure."

Now don't rush out and buy a baseball cap, but do protect your brain. Bureaucracies (can you say the College Board?) create nightmares for individuals like you. That's what they do. Accept that.

When you first heard, "It's not your aptitude but your attitude," you may have bitten your lip. Unclench. Cynicism don't feed the bulldog.

To defend his plan B, Cheswick clings to the fact that news anchor Peter Jennings dropped out of high school. The truth is, for most students, dropping out is the anchor.

Tell Your Truth

At age forty-two, Gilda Radner lost her battle with ovarian cancer. One of the original cast members of "Saturday Night Live," Radner was the sweetheart of Saturday nights. Her characters—the brash Roseanne Roseannadanna, the nerdy Lisa Loopner, and the misinformed Emily Litella—are part of her legacy. Radner was warm, big-hearted, courageous, and real—all qualities that you should aspire to in your writing.

Shortly before her death, she wrote a personal account of her struggle with cancer. She told the truth with the same courage she brought to performing. Radner was fearless: from shoving beans up her nose to hurling herself against a wall with rib cage–breaking force. Alan Zweibel, an "SNL" writer who published the memoir *Bunny Bunny* about their fourteen-year friendship, said, "She was accessible. She wasn't overly pretty. . . . It was just someone laying themselves out there saying, 'This is me. Like me. This is me. I'm gonna make you laugh now,' like a kid would."

In your SAT essay, you have to put yourself out there. Be unafraid. Tell the truth. As Radner's character Roseanne Roseannadanna would remind us, "It's always something." Now search your memory for the "somethings" of your life. Here are two suggestions:

1. Recycle Your Best "Somethings"

What makes a "something" into something good? Truth is the first requirement for good writing. Composer George Gershwin was once asked how long it took him to write *Rhapsody in Blue*. He replied, "All my life." Like Gershwin, your truth is shaped by every experience you've ever had. It's the way you tell what happened, though, that matters. A common experience can be described in language that makes it memorable.

Author Wallace Stegner calls this writing the "dramatization of belief." In her introduction to *The Best American Nonrequired Reading 2003*, the delightful Zadie Smith explains what Stegner meant. When you put pencil to paper, you "dramatize your belief in the miraculous, incommensurable existence of a society of six billion individuals. One of whom died three hundred and seventy-seven years ago while trying to freeze a chicken."

In this excerpt from a student essay, Reah Johnson addresses the topic "The Dumbing Down of America." Her "dramatization of belief" was written to be used as an original oratory in speech competition. Although she had already taken the SAT, Johnson's essay/oratory is an excellent example of how telling the truth about a common experience can make you more "likable." And, oddly enough, no chickens were killed (or frozen) in her dramatization.

Sunday, October 15. I am at the mall with a mission. No, not jeans, ice cream, CDs or cute boys. I am there to figure out the next four years of my academic life. Hundreds of booths are set up, each with eager college representatives passing out pamphlets, pinpointing information, and propagandizing anything pertaining to their school. It was the College Fair, but fair it wasn't. Some booths couldn't attract a single soul.

Being the clueless person that I am, I must have picked up a hundred pamphlets. It was at the end of my trek, though, when away from the mainstream I noticed *the* booth. Crowded with so many teens that I initially thought *Must be a party school.* I had to see for myself. Fighting through mobs of teenage girls and their mothers, I squinted to make out the university's name. "CLINIQUE

BONUS TIME." Not a renowned university, but a universally known cosmetics line.

Instead of learning about, say, the University of Michigan application process, the girls had chosen to learn about the application of "Sheer Sable" blush. It shouldn't come as a surprise, then, that media researcher Jean Kilbourne tells us the number one wish for girls ages eleven to seventeen is to be . . . on their high school speech team. You don't believe me, do you? Actually, what they really want has nothing to do with matters academic. They just want to be thinner. And, naturally, the number one wish for boys is to have a girlfriend who's well informed. . . . Did I say well informed? I meant to say well formed.

According to author Steve Allen, Americans are suffering from a mental incapacitation, and he's not talking only about teenage boys and girls. To be blunt, too many of us have become what H. L. Mencken refers to as the "Boobus Americanus," a bird too ignorant to know which way to fly. Well, it's time to wake up and fly right. Take a recent survey that revealed twelve-year-olds could name 5.2 alcoholic beverages but only 4.8 presidents. A third of high school students didn't know the United States had ever been involved in a war with Vietnam. Twenty-six percent of high school graduates couldn't identify Mexico on a map. And if you really want to be shocked, I could share with you my SAT scores. But then I would begin to cry and my new Clinique mascara would start to run.

Johnson's self-effacing humor (about her SAT score) and her playfulness with language increase her likability. But the true story of her visit to a College Fair is compelling—as an argument—because of the sources she quotes and the factual support she includes. And, let's face it, she is refreshingly honest.

Although it is unlikely that you will have much in the way of facts or quotes in your SAT essay, don't substitute goo for Google.

Avoid what is known as "sky is blue" evidence: for example, quoting the president of the United States saying, "Drug abuse is bad." Overstating the obvious is bad. When in doubt, stick with likable.

2. Stockpile the "Somethings" of Others

You may not have a relevant personal experience to share on a particular topic. What then? That's when you turn to the true story of someone else. You hear stories every day—from your parents, your teachers, your friends. The key is not only to stockpile those stories but also to remember the specific details that give the stories life.

In this student essay, Yasmin Mashhoon writes on the topic "The Media as a Freak Show." Her argument became that the media, too often, reflects who we are.

> I was sitting in English class the other day and my teacher told us a story about his days as a student at the University of Nebraska. Somewhat bored one day, he said, he was lurking in the lunch line at Selleck Quadrangle. So, in order to entertain his friends and the girls behind them, he was doing his best—or should I say, his worst—impression of a mentally challenged person. He was successfully distorting his voice, face, and body when he looked up for a moment, and his eyes locked onto those of a member of the kitchen staff. My teacher described how he felt her eyes pierce right through him, and she said: "How would you feel if you really were that way?"
>
> My teacher was immediately ashamed and he didn't say another word. Standing in that line all those years ago, he was ashamed that he was imitating someone different than he. At that moment, he made a personal decision to stop supporting the Freak Show.

Does the story ring true? Why? Perhaps because the details are not ones that would typically occur to a high school student. SAT readers are likely to react positively to this story both because of its uniqueness and because they want it to be true. You want an SAT reader to like you—to root for you.

The savvy student knows that the stories of others can be a valuable resource. After all, Gilda Radner's hyper pajama party characters were drawn, in part, from the work of Lily Tomlin's six-year-old alter ego Edith Ann. "And that's," as Edith Ann liked to say, "the truth."

Connect the Dots

"When you're acting, you ideally are out of control. In control of being out of control. And when you are directing, you should be in control. Somewhat out of control of being in control. But in control. And if you're trying to be out of control and somewhat in control of being out of control but out of control and, at the same time, in control but somewhat out of control of being in control but still in control, it makes you crazy."
—actor Warren Beatty, quoted in Bill Zehme's book *Intimate Strangers*

Beatty's convoluted logic notwithstanding, control matters. In writing persuasively, you need to have control of your arguments. You exercise this control by the choices you make. Those choices allow you to "connect the dots" in your essay. The process of "connecting the dots" means providing information, paying attention to it, and making sense of it. In short, you are giving form to arguments.

In discussing how to develop arguments, Aristotle said there are three ways to appeal to an audience: logical, emotional, and ethical proof. Of course, Aristotle was describing the art of public speaking. The principles, though, are just as important when you are trying to "connect the dots" as a writer. In other words, our persuasive power depends on our ability to reason, the emotions we are able to stir in the reader, and the reader's understanding of our character.

Logical Proof

You offer logical proof when you use sequence and analysis in your organizational pattern and factual evidence to prove your position. You are letting the reader in on how your thoughts connect. In the following passage, the student Ladan Jafari argues that the diet industry is taking control of too many lives.

Just pick up a magazine like *YM*, which, with no sense of irony, stands for young and modern. Throughout each issue the young and modern reader is subjected to the waiflike appearance of every model pictured. Kate Moss, for example, seems to be famous only for her skin and bones. And not surprisingly, in the last few pages of every issue there are series of advertisements about how to be a model, how to get "stronger, thicker, longer hair," and, of course, how to lose weight.

One weight-loss advertisement in particular caught my eye. For only twelve dollars you can own the Body Maker. The Body Maker promises: "Before you know it, you'll be going to the mall to get that cute bikini you always wished you could wear." Just ask Eve, a thirteen-year-old who writes to tell the Body Maker company: "Your product is awesome! I used to weigh 135 pounds. Now I weigh 115 pounds and still going down. Thank you for giving me my life back."

Guess what, Eve. You still need a life.

So how does Jafari "connect the dots"? Specific examples. Statistics. Satire. Are you persuaded by her approach? Is the proof logical to you? What about an SAT essay reader staring at a computer screen, eyes glazed over, nibbling on Krispy Kremes? In the immortal words of comic and author Spike Milligan: "Gobble gobble glup glup munch munch munch."

"You've got to want to connect the dots, Mr. Michaelson."

Emotional Proof

You offer emotional proof when you "strike a chord" in your reader by appealing to a sense of patriotism, family, justice, or the like. Risks come with emotional appeals. The reader might think you are silly or superficial. The traditional advice to young writers has never been more true: show, don't tell. Study this example from Molly Dunn, a student writing on the topic "Now is the time to rehumanize America."

> When I was a fifth grader at S.Y. Jackson Elementary School, my best friend Sarah was the typical nerd. One day, when the teacher was out of the room for a while, the class bully decided it would be fun to lock Sarah out of the classroom. As her best friend, I could not stand by and

let this happen. I stood outside, locked out of the classroom with her. Sarah was so hurt by the bully's actions that she was bawling. Then, one by one, my entire class came outside to stand with us. This experience was a lesson that I never would have received had I been attending school through my home computer. Sitting at a computer all day, a child might learn to read, write, and recite multiplication tables, but she will be estranged from the world of other children.

Do you think that Dunn's story would "strike a chord" with most readers? What percentage of English teachers (the readers of the SAT essay) do you think were bullied at some time during their childhood? On the other hand, what if Dunn had written the following:

Bullies often hurt people's feelings. They shouldn't be allowed to pick on people. If we allow this brutish behavior to continue, it will make us less human.

....

Ethical Proof

Lack of specificity weakens writing. Concrete details empower. Dunn's story about Sarah and the bully serves as ethical proof for the student writer as well. You offer ethical (or personal) proof when you show the reader that you have a natural honesty about you. The reader must sense a strong value system and an unwillingness to compromise when it comes to doing the right thing.

In the following excerpt from a student essay, Amaris Singer explains the need to "connect the dots" in our thinking. The ethical proof comes both from her extensive knowledge of the subject matter and from the clear sense that, to her, doing what is right matters.

Recently, I visited the Chicago Art Institute, and I came upon one of my favorite paintings, George Seurat's *Sunday Afternoon on the Island of La Grande Jatte.* As a nineteenth-century French neo-impressionist, Seurat's development of pointillism changed the way we view the world. If you stand a few inches away from the painting, you can see dots of pure color juxtaposed on a white canvas. But if you move away from the painting, you learn Seurat's true intention. His primary concern was linear perspective, how the dots connected and their relationship to the accumulated shadows that surrounded them. We need to see those connections. Our government agencies should connect the dots that surround them. Investors and businesses should be wary of dots that look too good to be true. And each of us, as individuals, must step back and see the big picture.

After you have completed any piece of writing, you, too, need to step back and see the big picture. Do your arguments make sense? Did you "connect the dots"?

> *"If a cat has kittens in an oven, does that make them biscuits?"*
> —Malcolm X

Get Your Backup

The author Richard Saul Wurman points out that "a weekday edition of the *New York Times* contains more information than the average person was likely to come across in a lifetime in seventeenth-century England."

How much information will the reader come across in your SAT essay? More than a Cro-Magnon man during his brief cave stay? Actually, your goal should not be related to how much information but to how good that information is. In some ways, the "Get Your Backup" strategy reinforces the principles outlined in the "Connect the Dots" strategy. The information that you provide to back up your position has to make sense.

Some have suggested that you write and memorize a couple of "general" essays in advance of the exam. You can then have those essays evaluated beforehand for content and correctness. The strategy is to pick universal topics like justice or freedom or responsibility. You simply apply what you have written to the specific requirements of the SAT essay topic. Warning: this strategy can backfire badly if your essay sounds too "canned" or if the links you make to the topic assigned are tenuous.

Remember that the readers don't expect a know-it-all approach. What they do want is one or two excellent examples. Make sure those examples are specific and memorable.

....

1. Be Specific

"All my life I wanted to be somebody. Now I see I should have been more specific."
—Lily Tomlin

Consider the advice of Jane Mallison, who has graded standardized essays since 1979—more essays than she can remember. She said, "Use specifics. So many mediocre essays are written decently in terms of sentence structure, but they say it blandly, or they don't give supporting details."

One student wrote about how America is becoming a "nation of spectators." She recalls a visit to Ellis Island. Pay special attention to her use of specific details.

I thought about what it meant to be a spectator when I traveled to New York last summer. I visited Ellis Island because my great-grandfather was one of the twelve million immigrants who passed through there. Embedded in the steel of the memorial, I found his name. And I remembered again his journey. To escape persecution, my great-grandfather left his family, friends, and belongings in Poland. He fled by riding through the night on a bicycle to avoid detection, and by hiding in the swamps outside of Krakow.

My great-grandfather loved being an American. But his life in his newly adopted home was not an easy one. He sold fruit, painted houses, and worked in a naval shipyard. He did whatever life demanded to make sure that his descendants would someday enjoy freedom. My great-grandfather would not have allowed me to become a spectator.

2. Be Memorable

As discussed earlier, the essay instructions will most likely ask you for an example to support your position. You should be collecting memorable examples that have numerous applications. A memorable example usually contains humor, action, controversy, or an unexpected twist.

Do you remember hearing about the twenty-seven-year-old adventurer in Colorado who became hopelessly pinned by a boulder? The boulder, weighing an estimated 800 pounds, trapped his right arm against the cliff face. The man, Aron Ralston, made a choice: to take his dull pocketknife and to cut off his arm—a choice to save his life. After describing the harrowing details in a gripping press conference in Grand Junction, Colorado, Ralston returned to his hospital room. *Sports Illustrated* writer Rick Reilly was there. According to Reilly, all that Ralston said was, "I wish I could have been funnier."

Is this story memorable? Do you think you might be asked to respond to a question that touches on a topic involving difficult choices? Does the attitude of the person making that difficult choice matter?

True, the SAT essay could be funnier. But, hey, you don't need a dull pocketknife to survive. A sharp number two pencil will do nicely.

Serve Your Sentence

> *"Like a superhighway, the sentence is a triumph*
> *of engineering: the stately capital letter, the procession*
> *of words in their proper order, every arch and tunnel,*
> *bridge and buttress is fitted to its job."*
> —Patricia T. O'Connor, *Words Fail Me*

Because you have little time for "triumphant" construction, you don't want to find yourself on a road to nowhere. Struggling to merge thought and topic. Searching for the next period. Lost.

The SAT readers consider sentence variety as one factor in evaluating your essay. Therefore, so should you. Use your ear to tell if you need emergency sentence repair. In his book *Write to Learn*, Donald M. Murray discusses the importance of writing with your ear. As a newspaper consultant, he explains to editors how he can pick out the best writers in the city room. Murray simply looks to see "which writers' lips were moving as they wrote." Of the two paragraphs that follow, which is more pleasing to your ear?

The ancient African Lesu tribe made boys dodge burning branches. The branches were hurled at them by their fathers. Then the boys were men. The Tlingit culture made girls live for an entire year in a dark room. The girls had to pluck and sew duck feathers. Boys in New Zealand had to kill sharks. The boys would venture into the ocean with just a knife. The Ubatu slaughtered wild boars. They used wooden spikes.

To become a man in the ancient African Lesu tribe, a boy had to dodge burning branches hurled at him by his father. To become a woman in the Tlingit culture, a girl had to live for an entire year in a dark room plucking and sewing duck feathers. In New Zealand, a youth had to take a knife, venture into the ocean, and kill a shark. And for the Ubatu, the challenge was slaughtering a wild boar, using a wooden spike.

(Please note: Today, such rites of passage may seem ill-advised. Yet every year two million of America's youth engage in their own barbaric rite. Herded into crowded assembly rooms, huddled behind tiny desks, armed with only two soft-lead pencils, these adolescents embark on a perilous mission: to choose the best of thousands of possible ovals as they undergo more than three hours of rigorous torture. That's right, they take the SAT!)

As you read the excerpts, you should have become aware of the importance of sentence variety. Clearly, the second paragraph flows more smoothly. The choppy sentences of the first paragraph make the reader seasick. That's why writers use clauses and verbals. That's why they combine sentences. They break patterns that might become boring and predictable. That does not mean you should crank out only long, complex sentences. Carefully crafted sentences are difficult to construct given the time constraints of the SAT. A well-written paragraph will have both long and short sentences.

Long before the creation of *Grammar Rock*, Ernest Hemingway took up residence at Conjunction Junction (that is, when he wasn't mass-producing simple, pared-down sentences). Hemingway imitators have parodied the sameness of his compound sentences.

And you can stop your story the way you stop a life and you do not do it and afterwards you are not sorry and all of which and none of which has anything to do with glory and honor and courage and booting empty beer cans in

Ketchum, Idaho, and the judgment comes and the compound sentence is served and sixty-two years become a life and then one day you run out of . . . "ands."

Even if you didn't know the term "compound sentence," you would realize that the repetitiveness of the Hemingway parody is too much. Learning the terms, however, should not be your strategy now. As David Byrne, formerly of the Talking Heads, said, "Facts are useless in emergencies." OK, Byrne wasn't talking about the SAT. But it is an emergency.

Take comfort. Chances are that the first thought, the first sentence that occurs to you will be your best. Writing teacher Peter Elbow calls this the power of "raw first-draft writing." Elbow believes that if you are excited and involved in the meaning of what you are saying, you need not worry. For the most part, Elbow is right. Worry is your enemy.

Your worst enemy, though, is the belief that you need to sound a certain way. That's when your voice, your truth, turns into "in sum, therefore, it can be noted that . . ." You shouldn't sound like a prisoner of pedantry. You should sound like you. Unless, of course, you're celebrity Jessica Simpson and you think that Chicken of the Sea tuna is actually poultry. Or that buffalo wings are made out of buffalo meat. Then again, hotel heiress Paris Hilton believes, or so she says, that Wal-Mart sells "wall stuff."

Remember: the ear doesn't lie. Nor does the mouth hear much. And the nose? Forget about it. But we digress. If you want to know if your writing flows nicely, your best bet is always to read aloud anything that you write.

"No style is good that is not fit to be spoken or read aloud with effect."
—William Hazlitt

Camouflage
Airy Persiflage

artoon legends Rocky and Bullwinkle befuddled a generation of young viewers with obscure literary allusions. Their self-effacing use of the phrase "airy persiflage" in an episode, for example, paid homage to another famous duo: Gilbert and Sullivan. In Gilbert and Sullivan's *The Mikado*, the character Ko-Ko asks, "Is this a time for airy persiflage?"

Ko-Ko's question is an important one for you to answer. Airy persiflage, of course, is nothing more than light banter. Empty chatter. You would like your essay to be something more. Something more than *bandying about boisterous badinage*. You should, therefore, incorporate literary allusions. Try to avoid relying, though, on lines lifted from light operas. The rarely used allusion should be just that.

The key to this strategy, then, is to choose a recognizable literary passage that will apply to a number of different essay questions.

Consider a line from Shakespeare's *Hamlet*: "There is nothing either good or bad, but thinking makes it so."

Here Hamlet draws the distinction between perception and reality. Hamlet knows that what is thought matters more than what is. In developing a strategy to employ this quote, it might help you to think about the three kinds of truth: your truth, the reader's truth, and *the* truth. In discussing almost any topic, after all, you can address the gap that exists between the perceived truth and the reality.

Study the following approach that includes Hamlet's line.

A major benefit of Prozac is the so-called placebo effect. Even if the drug has no actual physiological effect, the *New York Times* reports a high number of people who pull out of depression anyway. Some cases of depression, especially those caused by a lack of confidence, can cure themselves if the people believe they should be cured.

Doctor Hamlet would agree: "There is nothing either good or bad, but thinking makes it so." The *Times* notes cases of people who were really taking sugar pills and were cured, literally, by the name of the drug. Their "thinking" made it so.

Clearly, Hamlet's observation can be applied to many topics.

General Hamlet, for example, might argue that it is difficult to win a war without the people's perception that the conflict is justified.

Professor Hamlet might argue that people must "think" that teacher pay raises are warranted for those raises to happen.

Sports Illustrated writer Rick Reilly accurately explains the difference between perception and reality:

> *YOUR SLUGGER is a steroid-dripping cheat. MY SLUGGER has made a major off-season commitment to reshaping his body.*

> *YOUR TEAM'S FANS are the kind of single-toothed vermin that real vermin cross the street to avoid. MY TEAM'S FANS are fiercely loyal.*

Sportswriter Hamlet would agree, don't you think?

Four Tips

1. Select Not-So-Familiar Quotes from Familiar Sources

You may not want to rehash John F. Kennedy's famous "Ask not what your country can do for you . . ." call to a generation. That call has been trumpeted far too many times for freshness. On the other hand, if you are writing on an education topic, it might be helpful to remember Kennedy's less-known but chilling observation: "A child miseducated is a child lost."

2. Make Creative Connections

When you incorporate a literary allusion, you are connecting yourself to the reader. You now have something in common. If you can playfully strengthen that relationship, all the better.

Oscar Wilde argued that there is a lot more to stupidity than most people imagine. Reality television is going about the business of proving Wilde wrong.

This example has the delicious ambiguity of the Wilde witticism, plus it plays into the likely bias that the reader will have against reality television. And even an ardent fan of "Survivor" knows it's a guilty pleasure at best.

Now compare the following two sentences:

Critics were unkind in reviewing the plays of Tennessee Williams in his later years.

A crass menagerie of critics urged Tennessee Williams to take one last ride on a streetcar named retire.

The first sentence is merely correct. The second sentence makes a creative connection between his plays—*Glass Menagerie* and *A Streetcar Named Desire*—and the criticism of Williams by reviewers. Which sentence would be more memorable to a reader?

3. Tack-On Quotes Are Tacky

Avoid responding to topics with generic-sounding quotes. Contrived choices seldom survive scrutiny.

Winston Churchill once said: "Never give up. Never give up. Never give up." Similarly, I didn't give up when I was cut from the soccer team.

Ah yes, from Mia Hamm to mea culpa. Be careful of the word *similarly* as a transitional link. Chances are slim that the two situations compared are at all alike. Take you and Winston Churchill. Please.

Another example:

My friends often find it difficult to escape peer pressure. "To thine own self be true" must have been easier in Shakespeare's day when it was possible to "know thyself."

Avoid piggybacking overused quotes. Especially when one isn't attributed to the right source. According to *Bartlett's Familiar Quotations*, the advice "Know thyself" is taken from an inscription at the Delphic Oracle. Know thy quotes.

Martin Luther King had a dream. So do I.

Enough said?

4. Be Simple; Be Direct; Affirm

Never say, "In the words of so-and-so," or, "These thoughts were never better expressed than by so-and-so." Say instead, "So-and-so was right."

Beat writer Jack Kerouac was right: "Walking on water wasn't built in a day."

Sample Allusions Not Widely Known but with Universal Appeal

If you memorize ten quotes that apply to a great number of topics, you increase your chances for a memorable essay. Consider the following examples.

When you need to write about a personal hero or someone else you admire:

"She had never been especially impressed by the heroics of the people convinced that they are about to change the world. She

was more awed by the heroism of those who are willing to struggle to make one small difference after another."
  —Pulitzer Prize–winning columnist Ellen Goodman,
   referring to herself

For a topic that requires discussing the morality of a decision:

"Aim above morality. Be not simply good, be good for something."
  —philosopher Henry David Thoreau

For any topic that touches on hypocrisy:

"You can no more become a Christian by going to church than you can become an automobile by sleeping in the garage."
  —humorist Garrison Keillor

Now go find your own quotes. Search through your favorite books or pick up a book that collects quotes. Other sources to turn to are the many books that anthologize columns by syndicated writers (Ellen Goodman, Anna Quindlen, Dave Barry, and so forth).

Remember: in the military, soldiers wear camouflage to blend in with their surroundings. Literary allusions should dress up an essay without drawing attention to themselves. Does Dante need a brightly colored do-rag? Probably not.

In *The Mikado*, Ko-Ko's question was ignored, remaining unanswered until now.

Eenie-meenie, chili-beanie, the spirits are about to speak.

Yes and no.

Avoid Slang-uishing

B y the time you read this book, the schizzle will have lost its sizzle. Language evolves, even if you don't. What was once a simple kiss became "sucking face" became "tonsil hockey" became "tongue sushi"—a sort of cold rice kiss described by language guru William Safire as "a mutual rolling-up of teenage linguae engaged in lubricious osculation." Who says that romance is dead?

Someday, your inability to communicate with your children will frustrate you, the way your parents suffer now. After all, you're too young to remember a time when teenagers thought everything was "copacetic." And the beat goes on.

In fact, the average SAT reader doesn't know a nizzle from a nozzle. Is it any wonder that a high court judge in London recently ruled that rap should be treated as "a foreign language"?

Keep this ruling in mind as you write your essay. The College Board trains readers to consider word choice as one criterion in essay evaluation. They can't fairly evaluate what they don't understand. But being understood is not enough. You want to be appreciated, by golly.

Word Choice Matters

Here are four suggestions:

1. Just Say No to Sesquipedalian

You may be tempted to dabble in fancy words. Foreign words. Restrain yourself. The *New Yorker* illustrates how confusing tickling your fancy can be.

The denouement of the impromptu powwow convened at the accouchement of Sister Jane was that, Deo volente, the nuns would be separated by a thick purdah from that handsome young horseman Dick at the next gymkhana . . .

And we all know how painful a "thick purdah" can be. Or, at the very least, uncomfortable. Preferring long words does not make you a better writer—just less clear. Of the 701 words in Lincoln's Second Inaugural Address, 505 are words of one syllable and 122 are words of two syllables. Honest . . .

2. Yo, Can U Pliz Write English

Don't let the undue familiarity of online lingo creep into your formal writing. True, insider phrases and abbreviated words do fit into the electronic format. But the SAT essay requires appropriateness. Linguistic shortcuts, shoddy grammar, and absent punctuation may work with "sk8r boi" but not with rdr grrl. Or rdr boi.

In *USA Today*, Steve Friess told the story of a father who kept his children from chatting with friends online. Why? The father spotted a problem in his fifteen-year-old son's summer job application: "I want 2 b a counselor because i love 2 work with kids."

And would you like fries with that?

3. Practice Verb-Reliance

In his journals, transcendentalist Ralph Waldo Emerson mused on what it meant to be a good writer:

All writing should be selection in order to drop every dead word. . . . Then all words will be sprightly, and every sentence a surprise.

Emerson cherished spirited writing—the unexpected moments of delight that make us want to read on. But how do you create these moments in your essay?

Former baseball great Reggie Jackson once said of pitcher Tom Seaver: "Blind people come to the game just to listen to his fastball."

What if Jackson had said, instead, that Seaver had a really good fastball? Would anyone remember Jackson's words? You don't want your writing to be forgettable. So . . . *make high-energy verbs your fastball.* High-energy verbs push paragraphs forward. They add vitality and momentum (more sprightly than passive voice, Emerson would say). They shorten sentences.

She aced the math exam. (active voice)

The math exam was aced by her. (passive voice)

Don't assume, however, that passive voice is always wrong. Passive voice can create a more conversational tone—up to a point. In *The Comic Toolbox*, John Vorhaus demonstrates what happens when passive voice goes awry. Enjoy his description of a love triangle's tragic end.

Suddenly, the door was opened by the husband. . . . A gun was held by him. Some screams were screamed and angry words exchanged. Jealousy was felt by the man by whom the gun was held. Firing of the gun was done by him. The flying of bullets took place. Impact was felt by bodies. The floor was hit by bodies. Remorse was then felt by the man by whom the gun was held. The gun was turned upon himself.

The rest, as Vorhaus might say, was shown on "CSI."

Tip: don't overuse forms of the verb "to be": *is, am, are, was, were, be, been.*

Make strong verb choices. They should be striking. Unleash fastballs. Study the following passage from S. J. Perelman. In his short story "Farewell, My Lovely Appetizer," Perelman uses action verbs to move his detective around the city.

*I hired a hack to Wanamaker's, cut over to Third, walked up
toward Fourteenth. At Twelfth, a mink-faced jasper made up
as a street cleaner tailed me for a block, drifted into a dairy
restaurant. At Thirteenth somebody dropped a sour tomato
out of a third-story window, missing me by inches. I doubled
back to Wanamaker's, hopped a bus up Fifth to Madison
Square, and switched to a cab down Fourth, where the
secondhand bookshops elbow each other like dirty urchins.*

4. Find the Chiefest Words

As poet Emily Dickinson advised, you must choose "the chiefest
word, the best word." Choosing the "chiefest word" stimulates the
reader's appetite. In his book *The Elements of Expression*, Arthur
Plotnik discusses the stimulating words found in the menus of
trendy restaurants. Indeed, Plotnik provides food for thought.
Restaurateurs often find imaginative ways to take your American
Express card to its gastronomic limits. Otherwise, why would you
order "roasted ratatouille terrine with roasted garlic, garlic flowers
and virgin olive oil, Napoleon of dehydrated curly cabbage with
autumn forest mushrooms"? . . . yum-yum.

Furthermore, finding the "chiefest word" first can shape an essay
for you. Consider the following situation.

You and a friend linger in the candy aisle of your neighborhood
grocery store. Your friend furtively stuffs Snickers into his cargo
pants. You realize that the manager of the store has been watching
the theft and now heads toward you. As the manager grabs your
arm, your friend escapes through the front door. The manager gives
you a choice: you can either tell him the name of your friend or he
will turn you over to the police as a shoplifter. You think it over.
Betrayal or punishment?

Later, you want to write a story about this difficult decision, but
you wonder if there is a word to describe exactly what happened.
The word you are searching for is *dilemma*, a situation involving
two choices—both of them bad.

Such a word can be at the heart of successful writing. Take the Siberian dilemma, for example. In his novel *Gorky Park*, Martin Cruz Smith tells the story of a young gymnastics teacher in Siberia. While fishing on a lake, the teacher falls through the ice. The temperature is minus forty degrees. His dilemma: if he stays in the water he will freeze to death in thirty or forty seconds, and if he crawls out he will freeze to death immediately. He will be ice.

Smith writes: "He looked up at us; I'll never forget that look. He couldn't have been in the water for more than five seconds when he pulled himself out. But he got out, that was the important thing. He didn't just wait to die."

You, too, encounter many difficult choices in life. You are not, however, facing death in Siberia. You are facing the SAT essay. You can let things happen to you or you can make them happen. Learning to write well is the choice that makes words happen. Learning to write well is the choice to pull yourself out. It is the decision to take control of your future.

Now isn't that just jim-dandy?

Try Profiling

"Pure writing is the most rewarding of all because it is constantly accompanied by a voice that repeats, 'Why am I writing this?' Then, and only then, can the writer hope for his finest achievement: the voice of the reader uttering its complement, 'Why am I reading this?'"
—Steve Martin, *Fierce Pajamas*

If you read detective novels or watch television crime shows, you are familiar with the role of a profiler. The profiler analyzes data to forecast the day, time, and place a crime is likely to occur in order to prevent it from happening. You should be a profiler too. You already know the crime you are attempting to analyze. Unfortunately, the SAT can't be prevented, but there is data for you to consider. So, what do you know? You know why an SAT grader reads your writing: to assign your essay a score from 1 to 6. (The reader's grading system, or rubric, is discussed in the Practice Essays section.)

Do you really believe, though, that the readers are completely objective? With apologies to Pink Floyd, all in all, it's just another rubric in the wall. Every experience the graders have had—or haven't had—colors their evaluation of your essay. Suppose you write an essay on the topic of "love." If you asked the readers to define love, you would have as many different definitions as you had readers. Some would say love is affection, some, an affliction. And the images that you choose for your essay create in each reader an association with some real-life experience. For example, the image of a bicycle may remind you of your first solo trip to the grocery store. The reader may think, instead, of Lance Armstrong's battle with cancer.

And now that graders are sitting in front of their home computers, you may have to compete with some unexpected distractions: screaming children, reruns of "Matlock," a migraine headache. And, unfortunately, a reader is affected by the quality of the essay read before yours. Would you rather follow the efforts of the next Updike or the next up-the-creek? Chance and circumstance happen to us all.

So what do you do? As always, write the truth. Remember, at the same time, the strongest connection between writer and reader is simple humanity. The key, then, is to find the common ground. You may spend your every waking moment thinking about skateboarding. Believe it or not, the hired graders have other interests. On the other hand, rambling on about how you want to solve the world's problems makes you seem obsequious. You're against drug abuse. Now there's a shocker.

Keep in mind the advice from E. B. White discussed earlier in this book. Don't write about man. Write about *a* man. Rhetoricians have long known people are more persuaded by examples than by any other form of proof. They know you can lie with statistics. And testimonials are always suspect. But if something bad happened to Joe down the block then "dangit, something must be done." Apply this rhetorical wisdom to your essay. Write about a person. Simple humanity. Study the following two quotations:

> *"To be a child is to live in the fleeting joy of existence."*
> —former U.N. Secretary General Dag Hammarskjold

> *"What is childhood but a series of humiliating injustices that you spend the rest of your life avenging?"*
> —comedian Colin Quinn

Readers should be able to relate to you. Which of the preceding two quotations would you say better set the tone for your telling of a childhood incident? The correct answer is both (except for the vengeance part). You may write about a childhood spent on the outskirts of hope but always hopeful for tomorrow. Most SAT readers have experienced humiliating injustices. They would like to believe in possibility.

A final thought: grading is drudgery. The readers lose the desire to go on. Distress sets in. Countless essays come and go on the computer screen. And yet, the readers must continue.

Two Suggestions to Make Everyone's Life More Pleasant

1. Primacy: The First Cut Is the Deepest

You know the commercial that says, "You never get a second chance to make a first impression." From the first sentence, you want the reader to be thinking that your essay could score a 6. A secondary purpose of the first sentence is to get the grader to read the next sentence. If your first sentence isn't a "grabber," the grader may skim the rest of your essay. Consider the opening sentences from the essays that follow. Do they make you want to read the second sentence?

> *"Many delights have accrued from the recent plebiscite here, not the least of which is that we have elected our normal quota of dead people, Lyndon LaRouche followers, freelance fruitloops, and folks whose names sound like someone famous."*
> —Molly Ivins, "Political Asylum"

"My daddy down in Georgia told me, 'Son, take pride in your work, don't honk at old people, and never read a Civil War novel longer than Red Badge of Courage.'"
—Roy Blount Jr., "Shoe-Shoeing Lit"

"SAT scores are plummeting, college graduates can't read, and Americans are paying good money for bell-bottoms again."
—Bill Maher, "Are People Getting Stupider?"

2. Recency: We Were Kidding; the Last Cut Is the Deepest

Research reveals that we better remember what we read first and last in an essay than we recall everything in between. As it turns out, though, the last sentence stays with us longer than the first. The importance, then, of the last sentence in your essay can't be overstated. You should allocate your exam time so that your essay doesn't end in an unfinished sentence or an ugly smudge. The last sentence should round out and dismiss the thought. But it also should conclude your essay with a bang, not a whimper. You want the grader to leap from the chair and shout, "Huzzah! Huzzah! That essay was a real humdinger!" Or some such nonsense.

Read the following "last" sentences from professional essay writers:

"Seize it and let it seize you up aloft even, till your eyes burn out and drop; let your musky flesh fall off in shreds, and let your very bones unhinge and scatter, loosened over fields, over fields and woods, lightly, thoughtless, from any height at all, from as high as eagles."
—Annie Dillard, "Living Like Weasels"

"A man and his body are like a boy and the buddy who has a driver's license and the use of his father's car for the evening; he goes along, gratefully, for the ride."
—John Updike, *The Disposable Rocket*

"Apart from what any critic had to say about my writing, I knew I had succeeded where it counted when my mother finished reading my book and gave me her verdict: 'So easy to read.'"
—Amy Tan, "Mother Tongue"

Earlier in her "Mother Tongue" essay, Tan explains that she envisions her mother as the reader. Tan wanted to capture "what language ability tests can never reveal: her intent, her passion, her imagery, the rhythms of her speech and the nature of her thoughts."

Tan's mother will not be grading your essay. Envision an English teacher who wants to like you, to like your essay. Give the reader a humdinger.

F. Scott Fitzgerald was right: "You can stroke people with words."

Prethink, Methinks

"He was deeply in love when she spoke—he thought he heard bells, as if she were a garbage truck backing up. Her vocabulary was as bad as, like, whatever—but she had a deep, throaty, genuine laugh, like that sound a dog makes just before he throws up. He fell for her like his heart was a mob informant and she was the East River; she grew on him like E. coli and he was room temperature Canadian beef."

—Phil Proctor, *Funny Times*

A s you may have guessed, Proctor is making sport of high school writers. He composed his own essay with analogies and metaphors taken from the actual writing of students like you. Or should we say, like underpants in a dryer without Cling Free. So before you start writing amok, "proctor" yourself. But how?

Prethink Your Essay

The time constraints for the SAT essay make painstaking revision impossible. Even limited rethinking of what you have written will be difficult. Therefore, prethinking is probably your most effective strategy.

Before you put pencil to paper, take a few minutes to think about the assigned topic. Choose a central idea that you will formulate into a thesis statement. Then decide on related evidence and supporting examples. Now ask yourself: will the English teacher sitting in judgment of my ideas find them compelling?

If the answer to that question is yes, begin to articulate those ideas in outline form. Make sure that you have a clear thesis statement and that all of the ideas are connected to it. Don't write anything down until you have spoken the words aloud under your breath. Let your ear be the final editor.

Tip: practice prethinking essays several times before the actual exam. The most important practice session is the night before. Writing a complete essay under game conditions the night before programs your brain. In other words, sit in silence at a desk with a number two pencil. No music blaring in the background. No cellphone chats. No testus interruptus.

As you practice prethinking essays, ask yourself four questions:

1. **Am I clear?** The goal is not to hide your meaning in cleverness. The reader will spend only a few minutes on your essay. Vague thoughts or misleading information confuse the reader. Do you want a grumpy reader mumbling, "What the . . . ?"

2. **Am I precise?** Don't drown in the stream of consciousness. Are you saying exactly what you mean? The key is not how many details but how well chosen. Suppose that you're writing about your friend who loves words. What is missing from the following passage?

> *My friend is into crossword puzzles. Learning all those weird words makes him happy. I've never heard of some of them. Only one other kid in the school does crosswords. This very strange girl.*

Now read the passage from P. G. Wodehouse. Wodehouse names the people and provides examples of words familiar to crossword aficionados. Even if the reader knows nothing of these puzzles, the precise details employed by Wodehouse draw the reader in.

*George spent a not unhappy life . . . doing crossword
puzzles. By the time he was thirty he knew more about
Eli, the prophet, Ra, the Sun God, and the bird Emu
than anybody else in the country except Susan Blake,
the vicar's daughter, who had also taken up the solving
of crossword puzzles and was the first girl in Worcester-
shire to find out the meaning of* stearine *and*
crepuscular.

By the way, *crepuscular* refers to twilight, hence, imperfectly
clear. Hmm . . .

3. **Am I interesting?** Share your humanity. Write about people
as if you're composing music. No dissonance. Never off-key.
The sentences should please the ear. And the stories should
engage the reader.
   Study the excerpt from Lorrie Moore's short story "How to
Become a Writer." Although the passage is fiction, learn from
her storytelling ability. Give life to your true stories with the
same playfulness.

*Tell your roommate your great idea, your great exercise
of imaginative power: a transformation of Melville to
contemporary life. It will be about monomania and the
fish-eat-fish world of life insurance in Rochester, New
York. The first line will be "Call me Fishmeal," and it
will feature a menopausal suburban husband named
Richard, who because he is so depressed all the time is
called "Mopey Dick" by his witty wife, Elaine.*

Do you find the narrator in the story interesting? Do you
want to read more about her? Of course. The writing is fresh.
It flows. And the narrator is engaging. These are desirable
qualities in any piece of writing.

4. Am I genuine?

"Well, apparently that's what was missing from my other pieces, my opinions."
—Rory Gilmore, "Gilmore Girls"

When the character Rory reviews a ballet performance on an episode of "Gilmore Girls," she eviscerates the lead ballerina. Rory describes her as a hippo, and there is talk of kicking and wincing. The *Yale Daily News* then prints the review much to the dismay of the ballerina. The lesson for Rory, budding young journalist: your version of the truth can upset people.

Clearly, you don't want to upset the SAT readers. Arguing unpopular positions may impress your college professors one day, but rein yourself in for the SAT. You can't safely predict the politics of your readers. Their biases. Their open-mindedness. For example, you might not want to say, "You know, the Unabomber made a few good points."

We hope you are a good person (you were good enough to buy this book, weren't you?). Let your innate decency be at the heart of what you write. Elie Wiesel tells the story of a rabbi who said that when we cease to live and go before our Creator, the question asked of us will not be why we did not become a messiah, a famous leader, or answer the great mysteries of life. The question will simply be: "Why did you not become you?" When the time comes and you finally have to put pencil to paper, write your truth. Become you.

Take the Shot

t's 1998. The Cleveland Cavaliers battle the Chicago Bulls. Seventh and deciding game in the Eastern Conference championship. Three seconds to play. Cleveland leads 100 to 99. Michael Jordan takes the ball and dribbles toward the key. He pulls up from inside the circle. Craig Ehlo, one of Cleveland's top defenders, leaps out to block him, but Jordan seems to hang there in midair until Ehlo falls away. Then Jordan releases the sweetest jumper you ever saw. A video highlight for the ages. Forever known as "the Shot."

Bulls 101, Cavaliers 100.

And what did Michael Jordan say he thought about when he got the ball?

Nothing.

He just did it the same way he did it countless other times in his life.

No thinking.

Take heart. You may not be the Michael Jordan of essayists, but you have written before. Many times. We're not, however, recommending "no thinking." As suggested earlier, you would be wise to

"prethink" your essay. Just don't get caught in an all-too-common trap: if a little thinking is good, a lot must be better. Especially when those extra thoughts are not about the task at hand. Negative ones, for example: "I should have prepared," "I never do well on essay tests," "Even doctors have more legible handwriting," "I'm a bigger loser than Bobby Brady in that ice-cream-eating contest."

Don't give in to your misgivings. Based on twenty years of research on overthinking, University of Michigan professor Susan Nolen-Hoeksen suggests that at the first sign of a problem, you should pull away temporarily and then you should strategize. Because you have limited minutes to complete the essay, don't pull away for too long. You need to refocus immediately on the question asked. No mooncalfing. No lollydolling. Attack that topic with—to borrow a phrase from reviewer Robert Bianco—the fervor of a Soviet tractor documentary.

Dissecting each word in that question, though, can create a different kind of overthinking: the paralysis of analysis, some have called it. Laboring over each word in writing your answer can be equally troublesome. Endless ruminating is seldom illuminating— a lesson learned by Nicolas Cage as the character Charlie Kaufman in the film *Adaptation*. Charlie (in voice-over) ruminates:

> *To begin. To begin. How to start. I'm hungry. I should get coffee. Coffee would help me think. I should write something first, then reward myself with coffee. Coffee and a muffin. OK. So I need to establish the themes. Maybe banana-nut. That's a good muffin.*

Forget muffins. Learn, instead, from the experiences of writers gone by. When asked what he considered to be a day's work, Oscar Wilde replied, "This morning I inserted a comma; this afternoon I shall take it out again."

Now is not the time to lapse into a comma. Take the shot.

PRACTICE ESSAYS WITH ANNOTATIONS

"You're not the boss of me now. You're not the boss of me . . . and you're not so big."
  —"Malcolm in the Middle" theme song, by They Might Be Giants

OK, you're not so big. In fact, you still feel like a mediocre Malcolm in the middle of a muddle. You don't produce well under pressure. Or you have a lot of personal problems. Or you come from a family where cousins marry.

Well, you know the old saying: if you fall off a horse, fire the stable manager (or something like that). In preparing for the SAT essay, think of yourself as the "unstable" manager of your future. Stop horsing around. You're already good at that.

The stakes have been raised. These practice essay questions should help. They will help more if you answer the questions *before* you read the example essays!

Work with one sample essay at a time. Compare what you have written with both of the examples for each topic. The sample essays are not perfect. They were written by students just like you. Their purpose is to provoke thought. You need to define your weaknesses in order to improve in those areas. You need to shore up your strengths. You need to focus. Otherwise, you will share the fate of author Stephen Leacock's famous horseman in the short story "Gertrude the Governess," who "rode off madly in all directions."

After all, the SAT, whether we like it or not, is "so big."

Preparing for the Practice Essays

Warning: The development of the SAT essay is an evolving process. The prompts for essay topics may change from year to year. Don't let an unexpected essay topic cause you to lose confidence. No matter what is asked of you, your task remains the same. You must take a position on an issue and support it persuasively with examples from your studies and your experience. The question will always be open-ended and won't require any prior knowledge.

At this writing, the College Board was considering paired quotations as a prompt. The example below asks you to discuss the value of an education.

> *"If you think education is expensive, try ignorance."*
> —Derek Bok

> *"I think the world is run by C students."*
> —Al McGuire

This prompt allows you to agree with one of the quotations or to develop your own position that modifies or rejects one or both of the quotations. Your strategy, then, is exactly the same as in the practice essays: take a position and defend it with specific examples.

If you *always* remember what the reader *always* wants, you will *always* be in control.

The Readers Use a Rubric; You Should Too

The readers of your essay are trained to look for clear and consistent competence. The list that follows should be your guide as you practice.

- Address the specific writing task.
- Have a well-organized response.
- Include appropriate and fully developed supporting ideas.
- Have sentence variety.
- Include specific details.
- Employ strong verb choices.

Understanding the Annotated Essays

Each sample essay in this section has four parts.

1. Topic

No study aid will have the exact topic you must address on the SAT. All of the topics selected for inclusion here are similar to the modus operandi of the College Board.

2. Essay

Students just like you wrote the sample essays. You will be surprised by the shortcomings in some of the essays, inspired by the strengths of others. Learn from each of them. Apply what you learn.

3. Critique

An independent evaluator scores each essay. The feedback is meant to be representative of what a typical English teacher/reader might think in each case. Regardless of whether you agree with the comments, take them seriously.

4. Insights

The authors of this book added comments after reviewing each essay and critique. These additional thoughts should help focus your thinking about a particular essay.

Topic A: Essays I and 2

In F. Scott Fitzgerald's book *The Great Gatsby*, Gatsby is said to have believed in the green light at the end of the dock. This light represents, in part, what is possible but what has eluded him. At the end of the novel Fitzgerald concludes: "So we beat on, boats against the current, borne back ceaselessly into the past."

Assignment: Do you believe that we can leave the past behind? In an essay, support your position using an example (or examples) from literature, the arts, history, current events, politics, science and technology, or your experience or observations.

Essay I

In F. Scott Fitzgerald's classic *The Great Gatsby*, the title character, Jay Gatsby, is told that a person cannot relive the past, to which he replies, "Why of course you can!" Gatsby's certainty has at one time or another been our certainty, as we inevitably seek to reexamine, relive, redefine, or rectify the past. But while Fitzgerald believes that we are "boats against the current, borne back ceaselessly into the past," I believe that we can overcome our pasts by reengaging with them. That is, in order to leave the past behind, we must first face it head-on.

In American literature, the past is an essential element to understanding our notion of identity and our notion of the nation. In Washington Irving's legendary short story "Rip Van Winkle," Rip slumbers for twenty years before waking up to a postrevolution America. Rip is effectively ensconced in the past, as his own family, the townspeople, and the country have changed dramatically. In some senses, Rip was ahead of his time so it would not be impossible for him to rapidly catch up and live in the present. On the other hand, it is impossible to completely abandon the past as its very occurrence led to the present. Irving evinces this connection between past and present by having Rip discover a portrait of George Washington where a portrait of King George hung in the past. Rip made a decision to acknowledge the connection to the past in order to understand his future, and it is this acknowledgement that allowed him to leave the past behind. Similarly, we can leave our past behind if we at once acknowledge our connectedness to the past and the influence of it.

However, in an attempt to leave the past behind, one must be cautious to avoid being left behind by the present. For example, in *The Great Gatsby*, James Gatz becomes Jay Gatsby, and Gatsby completely ignores his past identity. Gatsby's romantic vision of his past with Daisy became an obsession for him, and he made nearly all of his social and business decisions out of a desire to relive his love with her. Gatsby emits a romantic hopefulness that is ultimately tragic, for in Gatsby's attempts to recover and relive the past, he loses touch with his present and himself. The flickering green light at the end of the dock, the impossible quest for money, love, and the past, ultimately extinguishes Gatsby. Oftentimes, fictional literary works are the most accurate depictions of society.

In examining "Rip Van Winkle" and *The Great Gatsby* we saw two different ways to deal with the past. Rip prefers to acknowledge and transcend the past by facing it head-on, while Gatsby prefers to escape from and selectively relive the past. In so doing, he loses his future and himself. Thus, in our own lives and in society we, too, are faced with choices about how to deal with the past. We can ignore the past, forcibly leaving it behind until it reemerges to destroy us, we can attempt to relive the past until we are destroyed by that quest, or we can choose to acknowledge our connection to the past in order to truly gain some freedom from it. In the end, while Gatsby's romantic hopefulness is something to be admired, it is also something to be feared, for it allows for too much idealization of the past and future, so as to make happiness in the present nearly impossible.

Critique

The author has produced a fine essay. She begins with an interesting introduction that provides a context for her thesis, and then she presents her thesis clearly. To support her thesis, the author uses two detailed and well-developed literary examples, and the combination of examples is sophisticated. Rather than presenting two redundant pieces of evidence to support her thesis, which is essentially a piece of advice, she demonstrates first the positive consequences of accepting her advice and then the negative consequences of rejecting it. Moreover, the author's language is advanced and fluid. She uses a variety of sentence types and a colorful and appropriate range of vocabulary.

The essay's weaknesses are its unjustified assertions and its failure to provide the critical link between the thesis and the examples. First, there are a series of weighty assertions. In the first paragraph she writes, "We inevitably seek to reexamine, relive, redefine, or rectify the past." She offers no evidence of the inevitability of such behavior. In the conclusion, she presents three options for approaching the past, though theretofore she has illustrated only two. The first option, according to her conclusion, is for us "to ignore the past, forcibly leaving it behind until it reemerges to destroy us." She provides no evidence of this in her essay.

Second, she does not apply her examples precisely enough to her thesis. Her thesis suggests that we must first face the past head-on before we can leave it behind. Then she presents an example of a literary character who has done just that and one who has not, but she does not adequately apply it to "us" or suggest exactly what we can learn from "Rip Van Winkle." She would not need to had she not promised it in her thesis. To get around this problem, she writes, "fictional literary works are the most accurate depictions of society," implying that Rip Van Winkle is a metaphor for the common man. But the incidental reference is not enough. The essay lacks the final level of analysis needed for its evidence to strongly support its thesis.

SCORE: 6

Insights

- The risk in attacking a passage from a literary work by discussing the work is that the SAT readers are English teachers. They think they know more than you. Sometimes they do; sometimes they don't. Unfortunately, they are the ones assigning a score for your essay. This writer clearly knows the book. After all, she remembers the line (not given in the instructions): "Why of course you can." English teachers somehow think their work has not been in vain when a student commits a passage from a favorite book to memory. The writer of this essay has won over most readers in the first sentence.

- Despite the criticisms of our hired grader, most English teachers would be impressed by the clarity and specificity of this essay. Two problems emerge as the essay progresses:

  1. The writer overwrites. The last paragraph descends into babbleland. In trying to make her ideas sound important, she generalizes in empty phrases.

  2. The writer risks too much in how she presents her argument. You need to concede other viewpoints when you are analyzing a novel that most English teachers will know intimately. Don't give them the opportunity to be put off by the certainty of your position. Don't equivocate, evaluate. Recognize the possibility of other interpretations.

Essay 2

Our experiences alter our brains. Every sight, smell, taste, sound, and touch running from minuscule sensory nerves are directed to our brains where fissures run deeper, cross over, and reconnect to accommodate the effects of our environment. Once we've connected a sensation with an emotion, given it meaning, it becomes a part of us that can never be erased. Once we've seen one child dying quickly of cancer, held his seven-year-old hand, and breathed in air saturated with plastic tubing and medicinal pungency, the experience is burned into the physiology of our gray matter. It then impacts our present.

F. Scott Fitzgerald's character Gatsby's path through life forced memories into his subconscious mind. Memories and experiences that are now etched into his brain connected with a web of nerve fibers that fire as a reaction. At the end of the book, he realizes that he no longer, or never really has had control of his future because it is so saturated with the past. His subconscious mind, drenched in life before today, allows for little variation in how he reacts to his surroundings. He cannot fully trust another because once he became drunk on reliance on another. He was deceived. And his brain remembers, and reminds him. He doesn't have to ask it to and can't stop it even if he wanted to. "So we beat on, boats against the current, borne back ceaselessly into the past."

Current psychological techniques can indeed help us to alter our thoughts and, therefore, our reactions to current circumstances. Cognitive psychotherapy allows consideration of thoughts, the ability to challenge them, and the capacity to alter the way we think about what life presents us. But where does the original thought—that our child may, too, no matter how unlikely, contract leukemia and die in a sterile bed, his body infused with chemotherapeutic drugs—go?

Does it disappear or does it change the way we act? Does it frighten us or hopefully incline us to appreciate the possibility and, therefore, embrace the present.

Our experiences shape us. Shape us physically, and emotionally. Every time we feel a song, or taste disappointment we become a different person. Maybe just slightly, or maybe in a drastic way. And as that changed person we continue to pass through life feeling in control of our decisions, and actions, unaware that we are really led by our past.

Critique

The author provides an interesting essay; she uses psychological theory to interpret Gatsby's behavior. In doing so, she presents a fine analysis of how our experiences shape us and how what we have learned in the past impacts the future. However, the essay becomes more an evaluation of a psychological theory than a discussion of the assigned topic; the weakness of the essay is the disconnect between the paragraphs.

In the second paragraph, she describes Gatsby as being so hopelessly caught in the past that he cannot really function in the present. She writes, "He no longer, or never really has had control of his future because it is so saturated with the past." In the rest of her essay, she describes something much more moderate, as summarized by the opening line of the last paragraph: "Our experiences shape us." There is a clear difference between our experiences shaping us and our experiences overwhelming us. She never reconciles this difference, and, apart from using some similar language, she does not make the example of Gatsby relevant to the rest of the essay. Moreover, because the author deals with the assigned topic so incidentally, the essay lacks a clear thesis that binds the paragraphs together.

The author's use of language is sometimes excellent. In the first paragraph, in particular, she uses rich detail to illustrate a poignant example. Throughout the essay, she demonstrates a fine command of sentence structure and vocabulary, and each paragraph is great. However, the essay lacks a central argument and real coherence. The success of each paragraph is not sufficient.

SCORE: 4–5

Insights

- The hired reader's assessment of this example exposes a common criticism of the SAT essay: subjectivity. I would have awarded this essay a score of 6. A reporter from *Time* participated in a mock grading session of fifteen essays on a typical topic. How many times do you think the fifteen readers in the session were in uniform agreement? Not once. The reporter gave one creative essay a 5; other graders gave the essay 2s and 3s (and one 4).
- Science girl's understanding of the human brain impresses. Unfortunately, the reader interprets the topic the way that many English teachers would. The expectation, even though the question doesn't require such discussion, is that the writer will talk more about the novel than simply addressing the stated idea in the passage. Science girl is punished for approaching the topic in an unusual way. The grader's critique may be correct, but it doesn't reward depth of knowledge. Or passion. Sadly, reader Gatsby, Old Sport, is not always that sporting.
- Despite the criticism of this example, you should try to incorporate what you know into your essay. Write truth. Care deeply.

Topic B: Essays 3 and 4

When in conflict, academic freedom in U.S. high schools ought to be valued above community standards.

Assignment: Choose one example from personal experience, current events, or history, literature, or any other discipline, and use this example to write an essay in which you agree or disagree with the statement above. Your essay should be specific.

Essay 3

The school and the community. Where do we draw the line? When in conflict, academic freedom in U.S. high schools should be valued above community standards.

For instance, there is often controversy over adding health/sex education to a school's curriculum. Community members argue that it is inappropriate for students to learn about the opposite sex's anatomy or sex in general. To them, sex is a "naughty" word that should not be in a teenager's vocabulary. I am sorry but it's time for these people to wake up and face reality. Times have changed. It's a common cliché to mock our parents for how they always tell us their famous stories of how they had to walk ten miles to school uphill— rain or shine. Similar to how this has changed, so has school in general, including the curriculum. Maybe older generations didn't have sex education in high school, but did their generations have as many teen pregnancies, sexually transmitted diseases, abortions, and deaths caused by sexual related activities? Sex education is not a fun, laugh out loud course where girls and boys get together and talk about teenagers' favorite pasttime—sex. No, it is a serious, in your face, here are the real facts education about sex that you had better know *before* you make any decisions of that nature. Sex education informs students of the realities and consequences of sex. It makes teenagers think about the other side of having sex—it's not just fun and games—there are such things as STDs and teen pregnancies. Sex is a part of life and growing up. It's not like this course will encourage students to go have sex—if anything, it will have the opposite effect.

In conclusion, schools should have the right to academic freedom. School officials are the most informed when it comes to academic matters—not the community. The community does have the right to voice their opinion and their opinions should be heard but should not dominate.

Critique

This essay begins well with a clear thesis statement and a potentially appropriate example. The essay's central weakness is that it moves away from its thesis in the second paragraph; the topic becomes sex education, not the conflict between academic freedom and community standards. Moreover, the quality of language is adequate but inconsistent.

The author begins the second paragraph by presenting the example and explaining that the community sometimes objects to sex education, thus suggesting its relevance to the topic. However, the author quickly launches into a condemnation of traditional attitudes toward sex education and a discussion of why it is currently necessary. She is more interested in talking about the intrinsic value of sex education than justifying it in the context of the conflict between the community and academic freedom. Moreover, because the author describes the issue of sex education as more of a social problem than an academic problem, the example's relevance is questionable. Finally, the example is overgeneralized, as the author does not describe a specific instance of sex education creating a conflict.

The author demonstrates a reasonable facility with language. She begins the essay with clear and precise sentences. As the essay develops, she uses a variety of longer and shorter sentences and an appropriate range of vocabulary. But the latter part of the second paragraph is plagued by a series of run-on sentences. The essay's conclusion, like its introduction, is clear and precise and represents good organization. Unfortunately the conclusion is not justified, given the second paragraph's departure from the topic.

SCORE: 4

Insights

- If you use a rhetorical question as an introductory device, make certain that it doesn't muddy the waters. A "line" implies separation, not conflict. Furthermore, an introduction that is not developed seems abrupt.
- You can tell from the critique the importance of staying on topic. If your essay wanders, you make it easy for a reader to assign a lower score than you might have otherwise received.
- Be prudent in your choice of examples. If you feel you must talk about sex education, remember that your readers may be more conservative than you are. You need to concede the strength of an opposing viewpoint.
- A condescending tone can be your undoing. Phrases such as "these people [need] to wake up and face reality" should be avoided (even if they're true).
- *Pastime* is misspelled. Anyone can make a simple spelling error, but proofread after you've finished the essay to catch as many as you can. After reading a manuscript with numerous spelling errors, an annoyed George S. Kaufman said to the writer: "I'm not very good at it myself, but the first rule about spelling is that there is only one 'z' in 'is.'" Don't annoy the reader if possible. Check for silly spelling errors.

Essay 4

Academic freedom in U.S. high schools should be valued above community standards. I believe it is necessary and fair to have the right to learn about many subjects even if the community doesn't agree. It is rare that every single person in a community doesn't agree with something, especially involving schools. To teach about things the community doesn't approve of is only giving students the other side of the story and allowing them to make their own judgement. Having knowledge of many subjects, even "forbidden" subjects, helps people be more understanding and helps the community in the end.

At my high school, it was not permitted to teach any sort of religion class. The school board said they didn't want to offend anyone. I didn't understand and still don't understand how learning more about my religion or someone else's religion would harm me. The parents of students—the community—thought we would be harmed by learning about religions, but now I feel I have been harmed by not knowing or understanding other religions. In this case it was necessary to offer as many diverse courses as the schools could afford.

Understanding a large variety of subjects helps the community. It opens our minds to new ideas and helps us see things from another point of view. This, in the end lets communities communicate more effectively.

Academic freedom in U.S. high schools should be valued.

Critique

This essay is clear and well organized. The author presents a definite thesis, justifies it in theory, and provides an appropriate illustrative example. She also probes the topic further, suggesting that favoring academic freedom over community standards will ultimately help both parties. The author demonstrates a facility with language and varies the length and structure of her sentences. The paper is largely free of mechanical errors, with just a single spelling mistake and one punctuation error (the correct spelling is *judgment*, not *judgement*, and there should be a comma following "in the end"). Errors of this kind do matter, but don't freeze up worrying that you might make a mistake. Hockey immortal Wayne Gretzky said, "You miss 100 percent of the shots you don't take." So write on with no regretskys.

The essay, however, would be stronger if the author had explored the central example in greater depth. The example can be summarized, without missing subtlety, as follows: the community thought that it would be harmful to teach religion, but in reality it would not be harmful to teach religion. Though the example clearly presents a conflict between academic freedom and community standards, the essay would have benefited from more detail. The author could have explained specifically why the community prohibited religious education, and then articulated specifically what the students had to gain.

Another problem was a too-vague description of community. In the second paragraph, the author defines the community first as the school board and then as the group of parents. Assuming those two bodies do not perfectly coincide, it is unclear which group imposed standards prohibiting religious education. Then the author asserts without justification that teaching a variety of subjects will help the community communicate more effectively, while abandoning her example. In total, the essay is good but needs a meatier and more detailed example to achieve its potential.

SCORE: 4–5

Insights

- Use the first sentence or two of your essay to provide an introduction. Give the reader some context or background to ease into the topic. Because the reader may resist your thesis (it should be an argument, after all), find some common ground first.
- State your case in positive form for a simple reason: it's hard for readers to process sentences with "nots" and "nevers." For

example, this sentence from the essay, "It is rare that every single person in a community doesn't agree with something, especially involving schools," will have readers scratching their heads. Did that mean that people usually agree or usually don't agree? It's hard to tell. Two negatives equal a positive; thus, "rare" and "doesn't agree" together turn the statement into a positive—apparently people do agree. But I suspect the writer really means that people generally don't agree. If that's the case, a simpler sentence such as "People in a community rarely agree on any issue, especially one involving schools" would be much easier for readers to process. Avoid stressing the reader.

- This essay does a nice job of showing the other side. When the writer mentions that the school board is concerned about offending people, she indicates to the reader that she has at least considered other points of view.

Topic C: Essays 5 and 6

The person who never alters his opinion is like

_____.

Assignment: Write an essay that completes the statement above. Explain the reasons behind your choice.

Essay 5

The person who never alters his opinion is like a wall. A wall is stiff, rigid, unchanging, and stable. A person who doesn't change their opinion is stubborn, close-minded, determined, and confident. A wall and a person unwilling to change their mind are similar in many ways.

A wall is stiff and stubborn, in that it is not going anywhere. It stands its ground. One would have to walk around it because the wall isn't going to move for anyone or thing. A person who never alters their opinion is also stiff and stubborn. He or she has their mind made up and isn't going to change it for anyone. They will stand their ground if it's the last thing they do.

Just like a wall is rigid and unchanging, a person unwilling to change their opinion is close-minded and determined. This unwilling person is rigid and unchanging in their beliefs. They know what they believe in and will close out all other possibilities and thoughts of others. This close-minded person is determined in their opinions. A wall is the same way. It will stand the test of time and won't change.

A wall is stable, and a person unwilling to change their opinion is confident. A wall also possesses some sort of confidence in a way, in that it stands there straight and erect, not to crumble. A person, so confident in their beliefs that they never change, is stable. He or she has a solid platform below them and it makes them stable enough that their opinions will not sway.

A stiff, rigid, unchanging, stable wall, and stubborn, close-minded, determined, confident person are unchanging in their form and beliefs.

Critique

The salient strength of this essay is its precise structure. The author presents her thesis clearly at the top of the essay, comparing a person with unchanging opinions to a wall, and provides a preview of the specific issues she will address. She then presents the issues one at a time, beginning each paragraph with a clear topic sentence. Finally, she restates her thesis and brings definite closure to the essay in her final paragraph.

A second strength is the language. The sentences are consistently clear and well organized, though the author is not very daring with her vocabulary. The only recurring error is pronoun disagreement; a typical example is: "This unwilling person is rigid and unchanging in their beliefs."

The weakness of this essay is that it treats its analogy much too literally. The author repeatedly makes the unconvincing argument that a person is exactly like a wall. In the fourth paragraph, for instance, the author refers to a wall's human qualities and a person's structural characteristics, calling the wall confident and referring to the human's physical foundation. She seems not to grasp the idea that in order for a wall and a steadfast person to be alike in some respects, they need not be alike in all respects. Each paragraph suffers the same problem: the author simply lists characteristics of the person, and then lists the similar characteristics of the wall, without really saying anything novel about either one.

An analogy is successful if it uses a comparison of two objects or ideas to describe a quality of one, in this case a rigidly opinionated person, in a way that more direct language could not. This essay essentially lacks the comparative element; the author describes two objects, the person and the wall, using the same direct language.

The structure is precise, and the argument is clear, but the analogy is weak.

SCORE: 5

Insights

- Avoid grammatical problems that might distract your reader. In the second sentence, for example, a singular noun (person) is matched with a plural pronoun (their) in "A person who doesn't change their opinion . . ." It's easy to understand why—the writer didn't know if the person was a he or she—but the fact remains that the person certainly wasn't a *they*. The solution? Make both noun and pronoun plural, as in "People who don't change their opinions are . . ."
- The words the writer uses to describe a wall are both positive and negative. This makes the reader wonder if the analogy is intended to be good, bad, or both. For example, *stubborn* and *close-minded* are negative words, as are *stiff* and *rigid*. But *determined, confident,* and *stable* are positive words. With these conflicting signals, the reader bounces back and forth—it's good to be a wall; no, it's bad to be a wall; no, it's good again. Be explicit about your intentions.
- As you noticed in the critique, some people will be bothered by attributing human qualities to a wall. Calling a wall confident, for example, seems odd to most of us. Instead of creating this disconnect for some readers, the writer could simply describe the wall in wall-like adjectives such as *solid, unmoving,* and *permanent.*

Essay 6

The man who never alters his opinion is like a roller coaster ride: turns and drops, loops and corkscrews, pulling the rider in all directions, but always ending up right where it started. Such is the path of a man whose opinion does not change. He may venture into the realm of original thought. He may explore the deepest reaches of ideas foreign to him. He may be towed up by the frightening incline to the impending drop, scream as he falls and flips and is nearly thrown from his seat and off the track that is his life. But inevitably he will find himself back at the boarding platform, perhaps shaken by his encounter with beliefs not his own, exactly where he began.

There is a certain comfort in knowing that the starting point is also the finish. Our unwavering friend knows how his story begins and ends. He may not fear change, but he fears the process of changing. He would prefer to stay his course, accepting life as it tosses him mercilessly from side to side, concussing his internal organs against the side of the body that is his means of getting to a conclusion. Other riders—his friends, his family, members of his church and his government—attempt to divert him. All who make his life what it is are contributors to his perpetually unchanging view. Knowingly or not, they are the architects and molders of the steel that becomes the path of his life.

This man may be a well-respected, productive member of his community and his world—a laborer, perhaps; maybe even a doctor or a scientist. His contributions are great, but they are limited by the constraints of time. Once he is gone, so too will be his gifts. They are defined by his estimation of what was, is, and forever shall be. They, like he, are stagnant and will soon be out of view. No matter what their scope and grandeur, they will be left behind because they cannot change.

If he is a doctor or scientist, he is the end result of the evolution of medicine and science throughout human history. He is last in a legacy of brilliant men who have looked beyond what is known and seen what could be. These pioneers, discoverers, and inventors who advanced their craft were never hesitant to change, to jump the tracks and see where momentum and gravity would take them. They were men like Louis Pasteur, who first attributed disease to tiny, invisible, microbes never seen. Pasteur did not fear the reper- cussions of his bold hypothesis nor the taunts of his con- temporaries. He altered his own opinion by questioning what was accepted as true. He changed the beliefs and strategies of physicians forever. They were men like chemist Antoine Lavoisier, first to accurately describe the process of com- bustion and clearly name elements like oxygen and hydro- gen. Lavoisier disproved the prevailing phlogiston theory, the popular opinion of his time. Instead, our doctor is the blood- letter of the Middle Ages. He never acknowledged the pos- sibility that disease is not caused by astrological tendencies and moral indiscretions. He is the alchemist, trying in vain to turn lead into gold. He is content to live with what he knows to be true, his opinions so painstakingly crafted, guiding him back to where he began.

This man will never experience a different ride, no mat- ter the line he stands in. He stares at the sign alerting him that he will be relieved of his drudgery in forty-five minutes from this point. All the turnstiles are the same. Every seat belt, every shoulder harness, every lap bar holds him firmly in place—to once again traverse the same circuit, each foray a little less thrilling than the one before.

Critique

The author's strengths are his creativity and his facility with lan- guage. He takes a risk with an unexpected analogy—comparing something stagnant to something volatile—but he justifies his approach and provides a fresh perspective on the rigidly opinion- ated man. Moreover, his language is supple and varied. By the end of his first paragraph the pattern of his language begins to mirror the physical movement of the roller coaster he is describing, an impressive feat. His weakness is that he thinks he is Khalil Gibran.

By the middle of the essay the author is more interested in indulging in overwrought language than in making any real point, and his analysis suffers. His descriptions are inconsistent. In the first paragraph he argues that the overly opinionated man "may explore the deepest reaches of ideas foreign to him." In the end of the essay he presents the examples of an alchemist and of a medieval doctor, describing both as if they never explored any ideas except their own. In the middle of the essay he suggests that the contributions of the opinionated man may be great, but he gives no examples. He then implies the opposite, by providing examples of greatness only among men who were willing to change their opinions.

Rather than providing so many examples, the author might have benefited from exploring a single example in greater depth, in order to apply his somewhat abstract analogy to an actual case. The thesis of the essay is constantly shifting, and it never becomes clear what the author's main point is. The language and the analogy are delightful, but the essay needs to be more coherent and more tightly organized.

SCORE: 5

Insights

- This essay avoids the trap inherent in the topic. A writer might be tempted to attack a particular person—a politician or religious leader—who the writer believes never alters an opinion. Instead, this writer extends the simile, introducing historical examples (that have no chance of offending the reader) later in the essay.
- The hired grader finds the flaws in reasoning, though. Most readers would probably not be that astute. The extraordinary facility with language and the remarkable extension of the roller coaster imagery would sway a typical English teacher to give a higher score. Still, you run a significant risk if you don't have a clear thesis statement and an easily recognizable organizational pattern. Remember: the readers are on a roller coaster ride of their own. And it ain't Disneyland.

Topic D: Essays 7 and 8

The door to success is labeled "push."

Assignment: Write an essay in which you agree or disagree with this statement. Support your opinions with specific examples from your personal experiences, your observations of others, or your reading.

Essay 7

My mother always told me you could have anything you want if you tried hard enough. This is the best piece of advice I've ever been given.

One sure way to succeed is to do what you want to do, not what someone else wants you to do. Is there something you've always wanted but weren't sure how to go about getting it? Sit down with a sheet of paper and list your goals and what you see as the obstacles. If the goal involves education, have you visited a community college or university? It often helps to get to know what you're facing when setting goals.

If your goal involves money, you may be surprised to learn that there are many resources at your disposal. Perhaps your employer has a tuition reimbursement program. There are scholarships. There is always financial aid that you don't have to repay until after your education is completed.

While your path to success may not always be straight, it is a path, nonetheless. You may have to take a turn in a path to accomplish your goal. For example: if you want to be a nurse but you aren't very good at math, you may need to take an easier math course before tackling a statistics class.

Whatever you set out to do, remember, what counts is your measure of success. That can be little steps, like taking one course, or big steps, like finishing your degree. The door to success is unlocked; all you have to do is push.

Critique

The author presents a well-organized essay and a convincing enough, if not very original, interpretation of the topic. She argues that the statement "the door to success is labeled push" means that anyone can achieve the desired goals if he or she works hard enough. Her thesis is followed by three focused paragraphs and a functional conclusion. Apart from two questions where declarative statements would do, the author demonstrates a good command of sentence structure, and she varies the lengths of her sentences for rhetorical effect.

However, the examples are sometimes confusing and generally unconvincing. The first two examples involve pursuing higher education. The author suggests that a prospective student visit a college and determine possible sources of funding. This is certainly good advice, and perhaps a necessary prerequisite to working hard. However, these examples do not explain how hard work will result in success and thus are not quite related to the essay's topic or thesis statement. The examples are potentially informative, but the author misses a critical link.

Moreover, some of the examples are confusing. The author begins the second paragraph by suggesting that there are ample resources available to anyone who wants money, setting herself up as a valuable adviser indeed to whoever who has resorted to scoring her essay. Then it turns out that by money she means financial aid, not an obvious inference at all. Another oddity is her suggestion that, "If you want to be a nurse but you aren't very good at math, you may need to take an easier math course before tackling a statistics class." To the layperson, it is unclear why the prospective nurse would need to know math at all.

The author's argument—work hard and you will succeed—is fair. The structure of the essay is fine, and the sentences, though not the vocabulary, are versatile. However, the author's choice and delivery of examples prevent her from selling her argument convincingly.

SCORE: 4–5

Insights

- Often you can find something in the beginning of your essay to repeat at the end. Doing so gives the reader a nice sense of completion. In this case the writer mentions her mother's advice in the first sentence. She could have ended the essay by once again saying something about her advice—especially in a funny or clever way.

- Be sure to consider other points of view. For example, "The door to success is labeled push" might strike some people as a bit harsh. It suggests pushy people or perhaps that the only way to get ahead is to push competitors out of the way. The writer seems to mean push in a different way—she could clarify her way by contrasting it with other possible interpretations.

Essay 8

The door to success is indeed labeled "push." None of the successful people of today just sat on their butts, eating fried chicken, and watching television all day long. The successful people today are go-getters, meaning most of them have really worked hard to get what they have. Bill Gates wasn't just a couch potato, Michael Jordan sweat his ass off for years, and all of the famous actors and actresses had to start somewhere.

Our world isn't designed for people to be lazy and still get the most out of life. Of course you could never go to college and work at McDonald's the rest of your life, but would you feel that you had achieved personal success? Probably not, and that is why people just like me plan to attend college, to achieve personal success. College is not an easy time;

it is extremely challenging. There are always those times when your friends are going to a movie, or to the best party of the year, and only you have a five-page paper due the next day. It takes a lot of willpower, but you have to push yourself to stay home and get it done, or it could damage your college success.

After college, oftentimes people enter the workforce to start a lifelong career. This career of choice is also difficult, and you have to push yourself out of bed every morning to do it, but you know if you don't do it, there may not be food on the table the next morning.

Success also requires changes, movement, innovations. If you just sit around waiting for the perfect time to create that new product or business, someone might beat you to it. In this competitive, ruthless world we live in today, it seems to be whoever pushes the door the hardest gets in and is most successful.

Critique

The author presents a very clear argument: work hard if you want to succeed. This is an adequate, though unoriginal, interpretation of the topic. Moreover, the author presents a series of relevant examples that illustrate the necessity of hard work, thus providing adequate support for her argument.

The author's facility with language is impressive; the essay is well paced and contains a good balance of long and short sentences. Where the author uses longer sentences, she punctuates them with well-placed commas, avoiding the drudgery of an excessively long sentence. One problem with her language is that it can be a mite colloquial, as exemplified by, "Michael Jordan sweat his ass off."

The author's primary fault is that she fails to develop her argument and her examples. Hardly an example lasts longer than a line, and all make exactly the same point: persevere and do not submit to sloth. By the last paragraph, the reader gets the point that working hard is a lifelong challenge and wonders if the author might have anything else to say. She does not.

The author has done something impressive in presenting so many examples. But she fails to realize that her point is so obvious that the reader need not be convinced. Because she chooses such a straightforward interpretation of the topic to begin with, it is not sufficient for her to simply restate her point over and over again. Had she taken a single example and developed it further, or examined a case in which hard work paid off in an unexpected way, the essay might be more convincing.

SCORE: 4–5

Insights

- The rater in the critique noted that the statement "Michael Jordan sweat his ass off" was "a mite colloquial." That's not putting it strongly enough. That statement is likely to strike most raters as rude and crude. The essay was appropriately informal with "Bill Gates wasn't just a couch potato," but "sweating his ass off" goes over the line. When in doubt, err on the side of caution—you can't unoffend a reader once you've made an off-color comment.
- The writer makes good use of repetition. The key word in this topic is obviously *push*. The phrase "You have to push yourself out of bed" creates a clever echo in the reader's mind.
- Be alert to the downside of any issue. In this case, some people might wonder whether being pushy is always the best solution. Is it really true, in other words, that whoever pushes the door the hardest gets in? It is best to consider your argument from another point of view, at least for a sentence or two.

Topic E: Essays 9 and 10

Pauline Kael, one of the best-known movie critics, once wrote: "The words 'Kiss Kiss Bang Bang,' which I saw on an Italian movie poster, are perhaps the briefest statement imaginable of the basic appeal of movies."

Assignment: Write an essay in which you agree or disagree with this statement. Support your opinions with specific examples from your personal experiences, your observations of others, or your reading.

Essay 9

What can be considered good criteria for a movie? Movie critics corrupt people's minds every time a new movie is promoted. Opinions and beliefs on whether a movie is good or not is something that should be treasured by viewers, not criticized. Yes, movie critics do help out in crunch time when a person wants to decide on what movie he/she should watch, but criticisms of movies only give viewers false criteria about what the movie may be about. Pauline Kael, a famous movie critic, once rated a movie with the phrase "Kiss Kiss Bang Bang." Pauline Kael gives a short but informative reaction on a movie.

The phrase "Kiss Kiss Bang Bang" states two major criteria found in famous movies: romance and violence. Romance and violence are two important notions that makes a good movie because it satisfies two worlds. First of all romance satisfies women that desire a love story in a movie. Second, violence satisfies men that want to go to a movie and watch cars exploding and gun fights. But how in the world can romance and violence mix?

The movie *Braveheart* is a great example of a movie that pleases a wide variety of audiences. Women love the movie because a man tries desperately to avenge his wifes' death. Men love the movie because while the man is trying to avenge his wifes' death there are huge battle scenes and warfare spread throughout the entire movie. Almost every famous movie presents the "Kiss Kiss Bang Bang" theory: *Top Gun, Lord of the Rings, Casablanca, Gone with the Wind*, and the list can go on forever and ever.

The "Kiss Kiss Bang Bang" statement given by Pauline Kael is a great example of a criticism of a movie that does not corrupt people's minds before they see a movie. Too many times movie criticism can vary between being two thumbs up, or two thumbs down. Kael's statement "Kiss Kiss Bang Bang" is a great critique that only lures viewers to movies, rather than scare them away.

Critique

Apart from the misplaced polemic that occupies most of his first paragraph, the author presents a well-organized, well-developed argument. The essay does not really begin until the second paragraph; the author's disparagement of movie critics does not relate to the topic or to the rest of his essay. When the essay does begin, it proceeds logically. The author affirms Pauline Kael's comment, presents his reasons why, and supports his reasoning with one detailed example and a series of short examples.

In the second paragraph, the author interprets Pauline Kael's remark, observing that *kiss* and *bang* refer respectively to romance and violence. Then he explains that movies with an element of each are widely appealing because women love romance and men love violence. The third paragraph provides relevant and detailed evidence in support of the author's argument, indicating that romance and violence, though intrinsically disparate concepts, have joined successfully in a wide range of movies.

A weakness is the author's language. For instance, he writes, "Romance and violence are two important notions that makes a good movie because it satisfies two worlds." The words *notions* and *worlds* are both imprecise, the sentence suffers noun-verb disagreement, and the phrasing is basically awkward. Each problem recurs. The author's description of the "wifes' death" is so odd that the reader wonders which mistake the author has made: was Braveheart Mormon?

The conclusion provides good closure to the essay, though the author seems to miss Kael's point, not recognizing that her comment was likely not intended to attract or repel audiences. However, despite some shortcomings, the essay is well organized and well developed, and the author successfully addresses the writing task.

SCORE: 5

Insights

- Sometimes we speak before we think, or in this case, write before we think. When we do so, we stand a good chance of putting our foot in our mouth. The whole first paragraph criticizes critics. Who cares? The topic has to do with movies, not critics. By the time the writer finds her bearings, we're already in the second paragraph. Even though your time to write the SAT exam is short, take a minute or two to first collect your thoughts. That can help you avoid a false start like this one.

- Be thoughtful about the words you choose. The word *corrupt* as in "Movie critics corrupt people's minds" is probably a stronger and more negative word than is intended. Corrupt actually suggests depravity or some kind of evil motive, when all the writer means, it appears, is that critics can sometimes ruin a movie for filmgoers. Tone down your rhetoric or risk alienating your reader.

Essay 10

Pauline Kael is incorrect in saying that "Kiss Kiss Bang Bang" is the basic appeal of movies. "Kiss Kiss Bang Bang" is an incomplete statement about the basic appeal of movies. While romance and action are the elements of cinema that are best able to grab the attention of potential moviegoers, there are many more aspects of movies that appeal to an audience. Action and romance are two elements that appeal to superficial needs, such as that to be entertained, but the experience of going to a movie also satisfies deeper emotional needs. People attend movies as an escape from reality, in order to fantasize about an existence different from their own.

Braveheart, a cinematic classic, exemplifies the appeal of movies. There is an abundance of action and romance to be seen, and these are the central elements in an epic historical drama. One could be entertained for three hours straight simply by witnessing the battle scenes and love affairs presented on screen. If that were all that *Braveheart* had to offer, though, it never would have gained the recognition that it has. The reason it is so acclaimed is that it succeeds in bringing its audience into the world of Wallace, in making them feel the struggle and passion involved with his life. The audience is enveloped in emotion as it is whisked away from a mundane existence and placed in thirteenth-century Scotland.

Movies appeal to audiences on a range of levels, from basic visual entertainment to deep emotional connectivity. A person leaving a quality film will feel that something has been learned, not just about a character on screen but about himself. The experience has allowed him to leave himself and his normal thoughts aside and enter a different world. "Kiss Kiss Bang Bang" might be enough to turn his head toward a movie poster, but he desires much more from the two hours he spends watching the film.

Critique

The author presents a clear and well-organized essay. He contradicts Kael, provides an alternative thesis, supports his thesis with a detailed example, and recaps his main points in a well-organized conclusion. The language is not flawless, but it succeeds with its clarity, and the author uses a good range of vocabulary. The essay effectively addresses the writing task.

However, the essay suffers from the occasional unsubstantiated assertion. In the conclusion, the author claims, "A person leaving a quality film will feel that something has been learned . . . about himself." This is trite, and the author does not give a compelling reason for why *Braveheart*, or any other film, caused its audience members to learn about themselves. In the first paragraph, the author argues that going to movies "satisfies deeper emotional needs." His only evidence of this, that audiences could empathize with *Braveheart*'s struggle and passion, is incomplete and unconvincing.

The author is convincing, however, in arguing that *Braveheart*'s appeal transcends the kiss and the bang. He argues that a film allows its viewers to escape reality, and how *Braveheart* did this by creating a vivid picture of thirteenth-century Scotland. That would have been enough for him to make his point. It would have been more effective for him to provide an additional example than to present additional claims that go unjustified. Nonetheless, the author presents a valid and well-structured argument.

SCORE: 6

Insights

- This essay demonstrates why clarity is the most important element in organization. The student makes a clear argument with sufficient support to impress the hired grader. The essay is easy to follow and makes sense (for the most part).
- It's a small point, but the writer shouldn't have switched from three hours to two hours in describing the length of film viewing, even though *Braveheart* was longer than most

films. Be consistent with numbers. The readers are in a daze already.

- The major concern is what is missing. The writer seems to have no personal investment as he describes the emotions of others as "they" are whisked away. The topic is discussed at arm's length. This approach may satisfy a jaded grader but fails to satisfy a reader who loves movies. When you write about a shared experience, don't forget to share.

Topic F: Essays 11 and 12

Cranky Mark Twain wrote, "Few things are harder to put up with than the annoyance of a good example."

Assignment: Write an essay in which you agree or disagree with this statement. Support your opinion with specific examples from your personal experiences, your observations of others, or your reading.

Essay 11

Mark Twain once wrote, "Few things are harder to put up with than the annoyance of a good example." Although, there are a lot of people that can annoy us by being a "good example," I have to disagree with Mark Twain on this statement.

First of all, Mark Twain seemed to be a very bitter man. He was an excellent author but was terrible at interacting with people. He constantly made comments like the one above. Honestly, I do not think that there was very much that did not annoy Mark Twain.

Second, people should worry about themselves and not so much about other people. Those who are annoyed by the "good examples" most likely have problems with how their own lives are going. They wish they could be more like the "good example" or even better: be one. That makes those people bitter toward the "good examples," which is led by jealousy. What these bitter people do not usually think about is they can make the choices that can make them a "good example."

Finally, I can think of many things more annoying than a "good example." For example: people chewing with their mouths open, driving under the speed limit, broken promises, lies, and getting the wrong order at the drive-through window at McDonald's. These things are many times worse than someone doing what is perceived as right.

Basically, Mark Twain was a cranky, old man that had problems with life. He apparently made many wrong choices that he wished he had not. Instead of trying to turn himself around, he chose to be bitter toward those who he deemed "good examples."

Critique

The essay demonstrates a solid organization and a range of argumentative techniques. The author clearly indicates in his first paragraph that he disagrees with Mark Twain's statement, and each paragraph begins with a topic sentence and stays focused. His sentences are well structured and clear, marred only by the occasional misuse of a comma.

In the author's third paragraph, he presents a somewhat detailed analysis of why those who are annoyed by good examples likely suffer from a personal shortcoming and therefore are not justified in being annoyed. However, the assignment demands specific examples to bolster the author's point. He needs an example in this paragraph both to effectively address the writing task and to make his argument more convincing.

In the fourth paragraph, the author demonstrates some creativity in enumerating a series of problems much more annoying than a good example. The author thus uses two convincing methods of argument. First he provides logical reasoning for why Twain's statement is false, and second he provides reasonable conclusions that are inconsistent with Twain's statement. In the second and fifth paragraphs, the author also uses a third, less convincing method: a personal attack on Twain himself.

The essay would be more convincing without the ad hominem argument and with a specific example to address the author's point about the relationship between being annoyed by a "good example" and personal faults. Nonetheless, the author delivers a well-developed and well-organized essay.

SCORE: 5

Insights

- A good example would not have been an "annoyance" in this essay. The lack of a fully developed example is more likely to irritate. As the critique suggests, the instructions require specific examples. The readers may penalize you severely if they believe you fail in this regard.
- The point about a needless ad hominem attack is important. Moreover, if you take potshots at Mark Twain, a beloved writer, you are making a huge mistake. True, Twain was bitter at times. Respect him anyway. Think of it, if you must, as kissing your weird Aunt Harriet. The whole family loves her. Guess what? The whole family of English teachers love Twain. And they should.
- Have a sense of humor. Mirror Twain's mocking playfulness in your approach. Twain also said: "Man is the only animal that blushes. Or needs to." Don't give the readers any reason to think you need to.

Essay 12

A grumpy Mark Twain once wrote, "Few things are harder to put up with than the annoyance of a good example." I must say I agree. Through my experiences, my observations of others, and examples in literature I will show why this is a statement that is true, even today.

First, one thing I can't stand is when someone is better than me. For example, music—which is my passion—is a very competitive area. Many people get egos and step on other people's toes. I think of myself, not as that person, but as a person who does feel a little annoyance toward someone who is getting all the fame. I know that is vain on my part, and I am trying to overcome it, but when you are good at something and someone else gets more credit for the same thing, you get a bit irritated. Little brothers are also a source of annoyance. I always feel a bit rough toward my brother when he does something well and gets credit for it, leaving me standing in the shadows. I'm happy for him, that's true, but I still secretly wish I would have thought of that first.

Second, by looking at my friends and classmates, I can see hints of annoyance. For instance, when a classful of kids have their hands raised, like people doing "the wave" all eagerly waiting to be called upon to answer a question, and the teacher chooses one who gives a perfect answer, there is a look of regret and loathing on some of the other students' faces. This is human nature in some ways. Maybe one guy wanted to impress the girl behind him about his vast knowledge of tree frogs, and today just isn't his day. There is also the ever striving desire to be on the top of the ladder. This comes from exerting authority and showing others why we are superior to them. It's no wonder why we are annoyed when someone one-ups us!

Finally, even characters in famous literature show annoyance when people show them up. To illustrate, the first thing that pops into my mind is *Harry Potter and the Sorcerer's Stone*, a novel by J. K. Rowling. In this novel there are three main friends, Ron, Hermione, and Harry. Of the three, Hermione excels in "book smarts." Ron is at the lower end of this totem pole. He is often disgusted with Hermione for showing him up in class and then trying to teach him how to do it "the right way," or really—her way. Another book that has characters who show annoyance at each other is *The Princess Diaries* by Margaret ?. In this series, Mia Thermopolis is found to be a princess in a foreign country. She is given a drastic makeover and her best friend, Lilly, doesn't know how to respond. At first she acts jealous, but in the end she is accepting and supports her friend.

All in all, through personal experiences, taking a peek at others, and looking at the library, it is obvious that Mark Twain isn't the only one who is annoyed with a good example. I attribute the annoyance to human jealousy of not having thought of something first or being lucky enough to have something happen to them. Next time I get a bit irritated with someone for doing a bit better, I'll think of Mark Twain and think of how far he got in life, even though he was a little bit annoyed.

Critique

The strengths of the essay are its organization and content. The author presents a clear and specific thesis statement in the opening paragraph, a preview of the body of the essay, and addresses the writing task adequately. Each paragraph begins with a clear topic sentence and proceeds by elaborating on the topic, while staying focused. Moreover, the author presents relevant and appropriate examples to support each argument.

However, the essay demonstrates poor sentence structure, a lack of facility with language, and repetitive and imprecise vocabulary. A representative sentence is, "I know that is vain on my part, and I am trying to overcome it, but when you are good at something and someone else gets more credit for the same thing, you get a bit irritated." Throughout the essay the author fails to use appropriate conjunctions or semicolons, or to simply use shorter sentences.

Where the sentences are shorter, they are often awkward. For instance, "There is also the ever striving desire to be on the top of the ladder." A related problem, exhibited in part in this sentence, is a series of poorly developed metaphors. Moreover, the vocabulary is repetitive. The word *annoyance* recurs several times and is often used awkwardly. In other areas, the language is imprecise, as in the author's observation, "I always feel a bit rough toward my brother. . . ." An additional problem is omitted details, as when the author does not know the last name of the author of *The Princess Diaries*.

The composite effect is a coherent but weak essay. The organization is strong enough so that the reader can grasp the author's intended points. However, the author's lack of facility with language, sentence structure, and vocabulary result in largely ineffective rhetoric.

SCORE: 3–4

Insights

- The critique suggests that the rater had an uncomfortable seat or a bad cup of coffee. He must have been in a bad mood when he read this essay because the writer has done many things well. The thesis is clear; there is a plan and plenty of good examples. That's probably a 5 for most readers.
- The essay has a surfeit of examples, in other words, too many. The writer makes three major points in support of the argument and provides not one but two examples to back each point up. That's probably one too many examples in each case. It's not necessary to overwhelm the reader with evidence; it's smarter to make good choices and present the best possible examples, one to support each point.
- Beware of clichés. The final paragraph begins with "All in all," one of a variety of clichéd comments ("in conclusion" is another) that tell readers they are coming to the end of the paper. Here's the truth: don't bother. It will be clear to the reader that you're wrapping up when you do things like restate the thesis.

In the immortal words of Zippy the Pinhead, "Are we having fun yet?"

About the Authors

Randall McCutcheon, nationally recognized by the U.S. Department of Education for innovation in curriculum, has authored eight books, including *Can You Find It?*, a guide to teaching research skills to high school students, which received the 1990 Ben Franklin Award for best self-help book of the year; *Get Off My Brain*, a survival guide for students who hate to study, which was selected by the New York Public Library as one of 1998's Best Books for Teenagers; and three textbooks for speech and journalism courses.

After nearly a decade working in radio and television, McCutcheon taught for twenty-seven years in both public and private schools in Iowa, Massachusetts, Nebraska, and New Mexico. He was selected the State Teacher of the Year in Nebraska in 1985, and in 1987 he was named the National Forensic League National Coach of the Year. Elected to the N.F.L. Hall of Fame in 2001, he concluded a successful career as a high school speech coach. In twenty-seven years, his speech teams won twenty-five state and five national championships.

James Schaffer is the chair of the English Department at Nebraska Wesleyan University where he teaches writing and journalism courses. He has a Ph.D. in English from the University of Virginia and has been frequently involved in developing writing curricula, assisting with a freshman writing program, and leading writing workshops. He is the author of three textbooks and numerous articles.

Schaffer was a finalist for the Teacher-in-Space program in 1985 and, as a result, became a speaker and presenter for NASA. He has given more than four hundred programs on the space shuttle to professional organizations, community groups, and schools. He was named Nebraska's Aerospace Educator of the Year.

As a journalism advisor, he has lead his publication's staffs to numerous state and national awards, including the Best Magazine of the Year award from the Columbia Scholastic Press Association. Schaffer and his wife, Mary Lynn, also an educator, have three children—Suzanne, Sarah, and Stephen—two dogs, and a cat.